Answered Prayers

Answered Prayers

REBECCA LAIRD

Editor

CARMEL • NEW YORK 10512

www.guideposts.org

Every attempt has been made to credit the sources of copyrighted material used in this book. If any such acknowledgment has been inadvertently omitted or miscredited, receipt of such information would be appreciated.

All Scripture quotations, unless otherwise noted, are from the King James Version of the Bible.

Scripture marked (NEB) are taken from *The New English Bible.* Copyright © The Delegates of the Oxford University Press and The Syndics of the Cambridge University Press, 1961, 1970, 1972, 1976.

Scripture marked (NIV) are taken from *The Holy Bible, New International Version.* Copyright © 1973, 1978, 1984 International Bible Society. Used by permission of Zondervan Bible Publishers.

Scripture quotations marked (NRSV) are from the *New Revised Standard Version Bible,* copyright 1989, by the Division of Christian Education of the National Council of the Churches of Christ in the U.S.A. Used by permission. All rights reserved.

"The Beloved Prayer" by Arthur LeClair, "A Little Like Lazarus" by Wendy Wilson Greer, "Gratitude the Heart of Prayer" by Elizabeth Ann Bartlett, "A Jail Chaplain's Meditation" by Lorette Piper, "A Tire Iron Parable" by R. Bruce McPherson, and "The Struggling Sea Gull" by J. Jerome Smith were previously published by *Sacred Journey: The Journal of Fellowship in Prayer* and used by permission of the authors.

"Calling Out Your Name" by Jim Cymbala is from *Fresh Faith.* Copyright © 1999 by Jim Cymbala. Used by permission of Zondervan Publishing House.

"God's Matrimonial Service" by Albert Gilbert and "We Walk by Faith" by Toni Grayson are reprinted from *Plus* Magazine by permission of the Peale Center for Christian Living.

Prayers from *Prayers for Every Need,* copyright © 2000 by Guideposts, Carmel, NY 10512.

"While You Wait" by Mathew Woodley was originally published in *Discipleship Journal* and is used by permission of the author.

Special thanks are due Mariam Ephraim for her editorial assistance on this project.

www.guideposts.org
Guideposts Book and Inspirational Media Division
Cover design by Monica Elias
Interior design by José R. Fonfrias
Printed in the United States of America

Contents

CHAPTER 3

Praying by Heart • 95

CHAPTER 4

Where Two or Three Are Gathered • 123

Introduction

Rebecca Laird

A book about *Answered Prayers* is ambitious. Co-founder and publisher, Ruth Stafford Peale, reminds us, "Whenever I hear some person say, 'God doesn't answer my prayers,' I reply, 'God always hears our prayers and He does respond to them, but His answer may take one of three forms: 'Yes,' 'No,' or 'Wait awhile.'"

"When our son, John, wanted to go to a certain seminary, I was unhappy—I thought it was too unorthodox for our son's simple trusting faith. What if these sophisticated teaching methods weakened his faith?

"So I prayed John would change his mind. What happened? God said, 'No,' to me. John went to the seminary of his choice.

"Years later, John told me how he enjoyed the challenge. 'You know, my faith was deepened and strengthened.'

"Yes, it was. Today, I'm so glad God said, 'Yes,' to John, and 'No,' to his apprehensive mother."

God certainly has long, hard-won experience at answering fervent prayers. Believe me, like Mrs. Peale, I know. On a dreary December day two years ago, my youngest daughter was diagnosed with leukemia. In a few short hours, we traveled from the pediatrician's office to the lab and eventually arrived at the children's oncology center.

Almost from the minute the diagnosis was delivered, people began to pray. My friends at Guideposts added their prayers to family, friends, and church groups. I knew that prayers for my child were being raised all around the globe. I learned to lean hard upon the prayers of others for daily strength.

For more than two years the life of our family revolved around daily medications, weekly chemotherapy, and regular trips to the hospital and lab. Cards and assurances arrived, and I clung to each one. A card sent from friends oversees declared, "Know that the beacons have been lit in Scotland." I propped that card on my desk where it sat for many months reminding me that bright, guiding, beseeching prayers regularly flashed near and far through the rain or shine, darkness or light found in my everyday life.

Often, late at night when I was numb with worry or fatigue and feeling spiritually mute, I'd check my e-mail. Without fail I found a note of encouragement, a word of wisdom, or a reminder that God was good and I was not alone. I could have never imagined the true comfort that could be carried through cyberspace. Even technology can be a tool in the hands God.

I have been a first-hand witness to a remarkable healing. My youngest daughter's health is fully restored. On mornings when I look at her sleeping face before she wakes, I breathe a prayer of praise for every new day we can share as a family.

Mrs. Peale worried about her son. I spent many anxious days caring for my daughter. We all know what it is like to stand before God with beggars' hearts to plead for those we love. It is our hope that as you read these heartfelt stories, you'll find encouragement to keep praying and waiting for God to answer your prayers. God is truly faithful to those who pray.

We begin this volume with the basic facts about Prayer Fellowship. Our promise is that every request received—by phone, e-mail, fax, mail—is prayed for by name and need. The result of our work is answered prayers, renewed faith, relationships with our readers, and that intangible change that occurs when people pray together. Over the years, we have become "prayer experts." We don't know exactly how it works, but we know it works. Some of the results of our experience are included in this volume.

We have poured over *Answered Prayers* sent to us by readers of *Guideposts* and visitors to our Web site. We've selected the very best stories on prayer from your favorite authors. Each chapter will deepen your understanding of the many different ways God answers prayers. *In Moments of Need* includes miraculous stories of divine answers during moments of dire need. *Ways to Pray* explores the many different kinds of prayer: spoken and unspoken, joyful and sorrowful, intercessory, individual and shared. *Where Two or Three Are Gathered* shares the blessings of group prayers. *God Knows Our Needs* reminds us that God does not always give us what we pray for: He gives us what is best for us. *Prayer Changes Those Who Pray* shows us how prayer makes our lives richer and fuller. *We Are Part of God's Design* proves that we can be the answer to someone else's prayer without knowing it and that God uses all of creation, even peacocks and beavers to bring about good.

We hope this volume will help you renew your faith and realize, as we do, that prayer really works, it works wonders!

Guideposts
Prayer Fellowship

Patricia Korol

Prayer Coordinator
Peale Center for Christian Living

Each Monday, John Murray arrives at Peale Center for Christian Living in Pawling, New York, seventy miles north of New York City. Along with two dozen members of the Peale Center staff, on break from their duties at Guideposts' Outreach Division, John, a volunteer, gathers to pray for the most urgent of five thousand requests that have arrived during the previous seven days.

Among the requests handed to John and others as they enter the room:

- Mary has three aneurysms and will see a specialist today.
- J.R. requests fair treatment at his Social Security disability hearing today.
- Bill will have open-heart surgery today.

At the same time heads bow in Pawling, Guideposts employees are also gathered in three other locations. Those sites include the headquarters in nearby Carmel, New York, the editorial offices in New York City, next door to the Empire State Building, and Chesterton, Indiana, where our children's magazines are created.

In all, two hundred requests are prayed for during Prayer Fellowship on this Monday morning. Each request is prayed for individually, by name and need, for that is the promise that lies at the heart of Guideposts' prayer ministry.

After the service, staff members return to their offices—to edit articles, plan mailings and make certain that customers get what they order. John, too, makes his way to an office. There, he sits at a desk, dons an operator's headset and presses a button on the phone. When the phone rings, he answers, "Guideposts' prayer line. How may I pray for you?"

During the next two hours, John prays for nineteen callers. He is one of two on the toll-free line at the time, and is one of thirty-five who staff the prayer line, eight hours a day, five days a week. (Thanks to technology that allows calls to be rerouted to remote locations, two dozen volunteers cover the prayer line from their homes.)

Most often, requests are for healing or for improved relationships. Among the heartaches John hears on this day is one that combines both problems: A mother requests prayer for a grown son who refuses to take the medicine his doctors recommend.

"It's hard for you, isn't it?" John asks.

"Oh, yes. We drove a hundred miles, but our son won't even see us. He has no confidence in physicians. Please put us on the prayer list."

"Absolutely," John reassures her. "Let's take it to the Lord. He knows whom we are talking about. Heavenly Lord and Father, we give you thanks for this mother's loving concern for her son, who struggles with anger and conflict. Lord God, help him to know that he is a child of God. Guide him to a doctor he can trust and confide in, and let him be healed."

It is the dedication of John Murray and the volunteer army of prayer warriors like him that enables Guideposts to keep up with the growing demand for prayer. Guideposts first invited readers to send in prayer requests in 1951. Today, Prayer Fellowship involves over one thousand volunteers. They handle ninety percent of the requests. Of the 199,260 received in 1999, 103,600 arrived via mail and fax, six thousand via the Guideposts Web Site, and 89,600 by telephone.

Those who visit the Guideposts Web Site (www.guideposts.org) can send a confidential request or ask that their request be posted on the Web site, to be prayed for by anyone who visits the site. It's not unusual to find more than three hundred requests there.

Among the most welcome letters that come in are those reporting answered prayers. One woman wrote to thank all those who prayed for her sister as she underwent a bone-marrow transplant and chemotherapy for breast cancer. "From start to finish," she wrote, "we were told that my sister was progressing much faster than the other patients going through similar procedures."

Those people whose requests cry out for more than prayer, receive a guidance letter from a trained counselor. In 1999, more than two thousand received such letters.

Among the most heart wrenching of the requests that pour in are those from readers of *Guideposts for Kids* and *Guideposts for Teens*. They tell about mean older siblings, divorce and death.

"I have this problem about lying and I want to stop. If you could pray for me, I would really appreciate it," wrote one.

Wrote another: "My mom dead of a drug overdose. Does it made me feel sad after My Mom Dead. The court split me and my brothers up. I miss my brother. How can I get the court to understane that I need my familie. P.S. God bless you." *(sic)*

Each child's request is answered by "Wally," the magazine's turtle mascot. He encloses a scripture, some advice and perhaps a story from *Guideposts for Kids*. In the more challenging situations, a trained counselor responds with a personal letter.

Prayer volunteers include active people and shut-ins, young people and the elderly. What the volunteers have in common is that they believe in the power of prayer and enjoy praying for others.

Typically, a volunteer receives a packet of twenty-five requests each month. One volunteer puts each request on an index card, which she carries in her car. Every time she stops at a red light, she takes a card and prays. If she has not finished by the time she gets to her office, she sits in her car and prays until she is done.

Every person who mails in a request receives an inspirational booklet, usually one written by the late Norman Vincent Peale, Guideposts' founder. One woman wrote that she had requested prayer for her critically ill godchild while the child's father was en route to Kosovo. The woman believed that prayers by Guideposts had guided the father to the child's bedside, instead. She also credited *The Power of Positive Thinking,* the booklet she had received, with giving her a comfort that she had never known before. "I don't know who sent me this booklet, but if I ever find out, I will give her a HUGE hug!"

Another form of comfort offered is a twenty-four-hour, toll-free recorded telephone ministry called Dial Guideposts. Those who dial 1-800-473-6188 can press 1 to listen to a different prayer by Dr. Peale each day. Or, by pressing 2, they can access one of seventy-six messages of practical, spiritual advice or press 3 for the number of our live prayer line. One million calls to this number are expected this year.

Twice a year, on Good Friday and again in November, Peale Center opens its doors for a day of prayer. On those two days alone, five hundred volunteers pray for twenty thousand requests.

One participant in Family Day of Prayer wrote: "I had to drive thirty miles on icy roads to get to Pawling. But as soon as I walked into the chapel, I was calmed by the peaceful presence of God. Seeing thousands of prayer requests stacked on the altar, I took a bundle of fifty. I sat down and prayed, 'God, look beyond my limited understanding of this, and just help these people, because they're coming to You for help.'

"Taking one request at a time," she continued, "I visualized the person, then thanked God for hearing my prayer and for helping that person." If a woman complained of pain in her back, for example, I would imagine Jesus putting His warm hand on her back and healing it as I prayed. Time and again, I thought, *If this person just gives his life to God totally, he will be all right.*

One telephone volunteer said so eloquently what is echoed by so many: "From the beginning, it has been a joy to reach out with loving care to those who call for prayer. Sometimes, I feel that I'm receiving more out of sharing with them, than anyone. But I have learned from experience that one can never, never out give our Lord."

It is the compassion expressed by this volunteer, but shared by all, that makes Guideposts' prayer ministry so effective.

Guideposts Prayer Fellowship will be fifty years old in 2001. We cannot guess the number of prayers we have prayed during that time, the number of people whose lives have been touched or the ways in which that ministry has touched our own lives, corporate and personal. We do know it is at the heart of what we do at Guideposts—and we believe it is at the heart of God, too.

Answered Prayers

CHAPTER 1

Those who love me, I will deliver;

I will protect those who know my name.

When they call to me, I will answer them;

I will be with them in trouble,

I will rescue them and honor them,

With long life I will satisfy them,

and show them my salvation.

PSALM 91:14-16 *(NRSV)*

In Moments of Need

Father, I praise Your holy name
for answered prayer and for prayer warriors.
At some of the lowest points in my life,
I cried out to You for health,
healing, and deliverance.
Thank You that during my times of need,
I was covered with a blanket
of prayer from Your saints.

Dorothy Bankston Adams

Prayer—
It Can Get You There

Ruth Stafford Peale

For decades I traveled with Norman Peale to his speaking engagements in various parts of the country. I met people who gave me new insights about prayer. One of the most unusual stories I've heard came from a woman in Atlanta who told me about working with God as her "space mover."

She had been deeply worried about a son living several thousand miles away who developed a serious drinking problem. His marriage had worn pretty thin because of this and there were the additional pressures of three children under five and a demanding job he felt locked into. He had an hour bus commute each way to work, and when he'd come back in the evening, he'd often drop into a bar at the bus stop near home. He never seemed able to get by that bar.

For several days, this worried mother prayed, asking God how she could reach her son and help him with his problem. *If I could only be there with him,* she thought to herself, as mothers do. *If I could only ride the bus with him and get him home safely each evening.* Then the idea came to her. Why not ride the bus with him?

So, the next morning at 10:00 A.M., when it was 7:00 A.M. in her son's time zone, she did get on the bus with him—in her thoughts. She rode in the seat alongside him from the suburbs into the city, sometimes reminiscing about things that happened when he was a boy and sometimes silent—just loving him and praying that he'd ask God's help with his drinking.

That evening, when he caught the bus for the ride home, she boarded with him again, riding beside him, loving him, praying that his early faith in God would be renewed. Twice a day, from then on, she'd remind herself, "Now's the time to ride with Dan," and then she'd commune with him and with God on his drinking problem.

After a number of days of this commuting with her distant son, she felt encouraged. Though it took a great deal of concentration, it also lifted her spirit to know there was a way, with God as the space mover, to be close to him. She kept up this commuting schedule with confidence that faith would work a change.

Some months later, visiting her son and his family at Christmas, she learned that Dan wasn't drinking anymore.

"You know, I have a long bus ride, back and forth to work," he told her. "One day I got to thinking about my drinking. I'd thought of it other times, too, but somehow, day after day, morning and evening, the drinking kept coming up in my thoughts while I was riding that bus. Finally, I made the decision to stop, and once I decided, even that bar on the way home didn't tempt me."

This Atlanta woman believes that prayer is a perfect vehicle—for communing and commuting—and I agree. Yes, indeed. Prayer can get you there!

Our Little Boy Was Not Alone

Wayne Kent

Leslie and I named our second child Benjamin. We liked the name even better when we read an Old Testament reference that called Benjamin "the beloved of the Lord, he dwells in safety...and makes his dwelling between his shoulders" (Deuteronomy 33:12, *RSV*). As soon as Ben started to walk, Leslie and I smiled at the wisdom of our choice. Benjamin knew two speeds—sleep and run. He needed all the protection he could get.

The November before Ben's fourth birthday, we were preparing to move from Tulsa, Oklahoma, to Decatur, Illinois. I had been asked to be minister at the First Christian Church in Decatur. One Friday morning, I was just about to leave for the day when our seven-year-old daughter, Jacqueline, ran into the kitchen.

"Benny's hurt himself!"

Ben's face was red and he was holding his neck. There was only a small mark, barely a scratch, on his throat, but his face was swelling before our eyes.

"What happened, Jacqueline?" I asked, trying to stay calm.

"He was dancing and hit his neck on the coffee table," she said, her eyes wide with fear.

Ben clutched his throat as he tried to breathe. "Daddy, make it stop!" His face was so swollen that I couldn't see his eyes.

"Mom, call 911!" I shouted to my mother, who was visiting.

Within three minutes Ben's facial features had disappeared, and the swelling had progressed all over his body, making him look much heavier than his forty pounds.

When the ambulance arrived, Leslie jumped in the front. A paramedic and I restrained Ben's flailing arms and legs in the back. As the sirens blared, we sped through the streets to Tulsa Regional Medical Center. Then Ben stopped breathing. "Pull over!" the paramedic screamed to the driver. "Get back here fast and help!"

The ambulance ground to a halt, and I jumped out to make room as the driver hurried to Ben's side. Leslie dropped to her knees on the side of the road. "We need you now, Lord!" she prayed. "Please help our son!"

I stood helplessly as the paramedics put a tube down Ben's throat to force air into his lungs. "Okay, let's go." The driver was once again at the wheel. Reaching the hospital at last, we raced after Ben's gurney into the emergency department, but we were stopped at the door of a treatment room. A nurse tried to guide us through a door down the hall.

I stopped cold. "I'm not going in there," I said. It was the room where doctors often told anxious families the worst, where I myself had tried to comfort church members whose loved ones had died.

"Please tell us," Leslie pleaded. "Is our little boy alive?" "Someone will be with you soon," the nurse responded gently. As we stood in the hallway outside that awful room, my heart ached for all the families I had sat with there. After what seemed like an eternity, a nurse told us that Ben, still clinging to life, was being flown by helicopter to Saint Francis Hospital's Pediatric Intensive Care Unit.

Leslie went in the helicopter and I took the car. When I arrived twenty minutes later at Saint Francis, I was greeted by more than forty friends, neighbors and members of our church. Mom had notified people about Ben, and that had started a chain reaction of prayer involving people all over Tulsa.

Five hours later we got the diagnosis. When Ben fell against the coffee table he had hit his throat so hard that his trachea had torn. Air from his lungs had escaped into his body, causing the horrendous swelling known as subcutaneous air.

After surgery to patch the tear, Ben was put into a drug-induced coma to keep him immobile while his trachea, still filled with a ventilator tube, slowly healed. Day after day, we waited and wondered. Would Ben live? Would he suffer brain damage? At this point the doctors didn't know any more than we did. But the hundreds of people who came to the hospital during those days helped us in ways the doctors couldn't.

In our panic on the day of the accident, Leslie and I had left both purse and wallet at home. But it didn't matter. Friends Charia and Mario Guajardo dropped twenty quarters into my hands, saying, "This'll come in handy for the hospital vending machines."

Our friend Jan Rohman kept talking to Ben. She took plastic farm animals and walked them up his arms, saying, "Here comes Mr. Cow saying, 'Moo, moo, hi, Ben!' And here's Mrs. Sheep and her friend, the horse. They all want to play with you, Ben."

Another friend, Dyanna Walling, slept in Ben's room for two nights so Leslie and I could get some rest in a room down the hall. Betty Calhoun from Fort Worth, Texas, who had had a medical test herself the morning of Ben's accident, drove five hours with her husband that same afternoon to be with us.

Someone tore the music and words for "Be Strong in the Lord" from an old hymnal and brought it to the hospital. A call came from our new church in Decatur saying that children were wearing "Ben Bands" on their arms to remind them to pray for our son.

We received cassettes of healing music and Scripture, sent by friends across the country whom we hadn't heard from in years. Schoolchildren from both Tulsa and Decatur sent handmade cards with bright crayon messages. One girl made a funny mask from a paper plate so Ben would have something to play with.

Six days after the accident, Ben woke up. "Mommy?" he murmured. Leslie leaned close. "I want to go to heaven," he said. "I want to play with Jesus and the puppies. There are lots of puppies in heaven." Thunderstruck with joy, Leslie climbed into Ben's bed and snuggled next to him.

Ben completely recovered and was soon released from the hospital. When Leslie asked more about his visit to heaven, he explained matter-of-factly: "It's like a big dog show! Lots of dogs and puppies!"

Benjamin had always been afraid of dogs, but not anymore. And when he saw Jan and Dyanna, he said, "Auntie Jan, you played animals with me. Auntie Dyanna, you sleeped with me."

Although we may never know what Ben experienced during the six days of his coma, I do know one thing for certain. Benjamin Kent was not alone. He rested between God's shoulders.

Nor were we alone. From the many people who comforted us, I've learned that being a minister isn't just about preaching a well-polished sermon. Being a minister is bringing a handful of quarters to someone pacing a hospital hallway. It's gently trotting toy animals up and down the body of an injured child. It's wearing a band on your arm to remind you to pray for a sick boy. It's taking up crayons to make a banner that shouts out a message of hope.

While Ben, "beloved of the Lord," was with Jesus playing with puppies, Leslie and I were learning that God is everywhere, not only in heaven, but here on earth.

Miracle Bookmark

Amy Love

My friend Stacy and I took our time walking down the hall to the library. "I don't know why we have to do book reports," I told her. "I like to read, but not when someone tells me I have to do it."

Stacy agreed. "I know what you mean!"

The truth was, doing a book report was the least of my worries. I had lots of other things on my mind. My parents were divorced, and my mom had applied for welfare. With eight brothers and sisters, life was sometimes hard. In fact, Mom had told me there was no money for the clothes I needed for school—so I was asking God to help us in some way. It wasn't easy seeing all my friends wearing nice, new clothes.

In the library, Stacy and I started looking at the books, hoping to find something interesting—and short! One of the first books I spotted was *Little Women* by Louisa May Alcott.

"Look, Stacy," I said. "This is one of my mom's favorite books!"

I knew it was too long, and that we had a copy of it at home, but I picked it up anyway and flipped through the pages. I couldn't believe my eyes when I saw the strange bookmark someone had left in it—a fifty-dollar bill!

I grabbed Stacy's arm. "Look what I found!" I exclaimed.

"Wow!" she said. "Are you going to keep it?"

I thought about what fifty dollars would buy. New shoes. New jeans. A couple of nice sweaters. But I knew what I had to do.

I took the money to the principal's office. The secretary was very matter-of-fact. "The money will have to stay in the office for thirty days," she said. "If no one reports it lost, you'll get to keep it."

It was the longest thirty days of my life! Finally, though, the month was up. The money was mine!

I know now that God cares about everything in my life—even new school clothes.

Out on the Lake

Howard Urband

As a boy, I spent summers at my Grandma's cottage on a lake in northern New Jersey. I passed the time swimming and boating and hiking—and occasionally venturing off on an overnight camping trip across the lake with my friend George. Looking back now, I recall summers full of boyhood joy and excitement. But there were also uncertain times. I did a lot of growing up at that lake.

One of those painful times was the summer my mother died. That same week, Dad took me aside and said he'd be going away soon. Because Dad was a schoolteacher, he had always been able to spend summers with us. But that was about to change. "Son," he said, as he held me by my skinny shoulders, "I've been ordered back to the army." It was 1940 and the prospect of war darkened the horizon.

Dad was assigned to airbase construction on the East Coast. During the school year, I stayed with Dad, but we moved around a lot and I felt rootless and displaced, always the new kid in whatever town the military sent us to. Summers I'd go back to Grandma's place, the one constant in my life. I missed my dad and mourned my mom, but at least at the lake I had friends like George, buddies who made me feel less alone in the world.

One bright morning I found George in his dad's workshop tinkering with an ancient half-horse outboard motor. "My pop has never been able to get it started," George explained. "He said I could have it if I can get it to run."

Perfect. At thirteen, neither of us knew much about recalcitrant outboard motors, but the challenge was too much to pass up. With a motor like this one we could take George's old rowboat way up the lake and camp overnight on a big flat rock along the uninhabited shore where Dad and I used to fish.

We disassembled the motor and cleaned every part, then carefully put it back together and installed it on George's boat down at the dock. We took turns pulling the starter rope until our arms were ready to fall off, but we couldn't even get a sputter out of it. In desperation, George took it off the boat and tried starting it dry. With no water resistance it roared to life. After the little motor was warmed up we shut it off and tried starting it on the boat again. Presto! The camping trip was on.

The sun shone off the glassy surface of the water, and I was reminded of the last time Dad and I had gone fishing. Dad had fashioned a fishing pole from a sapling and showed me how to coax the big ones from the shadowy places between the rocks. We had caught three that day and Mom had pan-fried them for dinner. Now Mom was gone and Dad was far away. Suddenly I felt so alone out there in the middle of the deep lake.

After reaching camp in the dwindling daylight, George and I hastily tied up the boat, then stretched a tarp above the camping area, securing it by ropes to the surrounding rocks. The open front of our shelter faced the lake, above the boat, which was moored between some half-submerged rocks that formed a natural slip. There was just enough room for us on the big flat rock. We rested quietly and watched the sunset. Heaven seemed to surround us. We took a moonlight swim and crawled off to sleep.

Around midnight George and I were awakened by the patter of raindrops. There was a slight wind, so we double-checked the ropes securing the tarp. The moon had slipped behind some clouds, and the lake loomed dark and ominous. The rumble of thunder reached us from the distance.

Before we knew it, the rain became a downpour. Lightning danced across the water. Huge whitecaps were being whipped up by a violent wind. Cowering under the tarp, we heard waves pounding our little boat. We crawled down and tried to retie it, but nothing could stop it from being bashed against the rocks.

Suddenly we heard a ripping sound. The tarp had split from the weight of water collecting on it. Our gear was soaked and we'd lost what little protection we had from the elements. We faced a tough choice: Stay and lose the boat and motor, or cross the lake and maybe drown in the effort. I tried to think. *What would Dad do!* I wished he were here to help me.

"If we don't get out of here," George called above the wind, "this boat will be wrecked and we'll be trapped!" We stared at each other. Would the engine even start?

I tossed our soggy gear into the boat while George poured the last of the gasoline into the small tank and set the choke. *Dear Father in heaven,* I prayed desperately, *help us get out of this.*

A flash of lightning illuminated George's determined features. He gritted his teeth as he grasped the starter rope. One mighty pull and the engine burst to life. I pushed off from shore and leaped onto the bow just in the nick of time.

Thunder shook the darkness, and the screaming wind ripped the foamy tops off the waves and hurled them at us, slashing our faces.

"Bail!" George cried. I found an old bait can under the seat and began bailing furiously. But the water was coming in faster than I could toss it out. Lightning bolts stabbed at the lake, followed almost instantly by earsplitting cracks of thunder. *The storm is right on top of us,* I thought, panic driving me to bail even more desperately. Where were we? How long would the motor hold out?

Again I prayed, *God. We don't want to drown. Please help us.* Suddenly my muscles loosened, and some of the panic drained away. I knew I needed to conserve my strength and work at a measured pace. That's what Dad would have told me to do.

The motor kept up a steady, comforting beat and I bailed enough to keep us from getting swamped. But still the storm raged. After more than an hour, George unscrewed the gas cap and dipped a forefinger into the tank. "It's almost empty," he said. "Can you see shore yet?"

I peered through the rain and dark. Nothing. If the engine died, we'd be swamped. Suddenly I heard waves crashing into the shore off to our right. "George," I shouted, pointing. "Over there!"

George changed course, and a few minutes later a splash of pale lightning lit up the familiar docks ahead. As we drew close we could see much bigger craft than ours had wrecked and sunk in their moorings. We beached our boat in the soft sand and dragged it, still partly full of water, as far as we could.

A few minutes later I burst into Grandma's cottage. She was beside herself with worry. "I've never seen a storm this bad," she cried, hugging me. "Thank God you're safe!"

The next afternoon I trudged through the rain to George's house where I found him back in the workshop tinkering with the outboard motor again. There was a puzzled expression on his face. "Look here," he said, jabbing his finger at the engine.

I saw what puzzled him. The nut that secured the spark plug wire to the plug was nowhere to be found.

"It couldn't have run like that," I said.

"I know," George agreed, tinkering some more as if he could somehow discover the secret. But I had already uncovered my own secret the night before, a secret to growing up. I'd found that no matter how alone I might feel, I am never truly alone. My heavenly Father is always present, a constant in my life, watching over me and protecting me. Soon I'd start school again in another town. But this time I wouldn't feel quite so out of place; I wouldn't have to do it alone.

By the way, that was the last trip George's outboard motor made. Despite his best efforts, no amount of tinkering ever got that engine running again.

God's Transmission Fluid

Robin Smith

Several years ago I was traveling from Salt Lake City, Utah to San Fernando Valley in California to visit my parents. I was taking my four sons but my husband was unable to make the trip this time. I invited two teenage boys who were great friends of our family to travel with us so I would have an extra pair or two of hands.

My husband carefully checked all the fluid levels in the car and the air pressure in the tires and also took the car into a local shop for transmission service. He was a little nervous about me traveling across the desert with only two fourteen-year-olds for help.

The morning we left I had prayer with my children before leaving our home. As always before a trip, I prayed that we would be kept safe and that the car would function properly. I felt an overwhelming sense of peace and protection, like warm molasses spreading over my body. I could hardly finish the prayer. Later, when we picked the other boys up, we prayed again with them. Again, I felt the warmth engulf me. I thought to myself, *this seems a little extreme for a car ride, but I'm glad God loves me.*

We made the trip in one day. It took about fourteen hours with gas fill-ups and wiggly child stops. As I pulled into Victorville to drop off my teenage helpers, about ninety minutes from my final destination, I could tell the transmission was acting sluggish. *But how could that be?* I wondered. *I just had it serviced.*

By the time I got to my parents' home, the car would barely shift gears and was making strange sounds. My dad followed me to a dealership the next morning so I could leave it to be worked on. The serviceman said that he wouldn't even look at it without a $100 deposit, because it sounded like such a serious problem. He also said it would take a week or so to fix. "But I don't have a week, and I don't have $100 to spare!" I told him.

"Well, then you're free to take it somewhere else," he replied. But I had no other options. I guessed I would just have to borrow money from my parents to drive home.

Later that day, the serviceman called back. "Your car is ready, and your refund of $25 is here also."

"What was wrong with it?"

"Lady, I don't know how you got here. You say you had the transmission serviced just before you came?"

"Yes, about two days before."

"Well, whoever serviced your transmission neglected to replace the fluid. You had no transmission fluid in your vehicle at all. It shouldn't have functioned at all. And I sure don't understand how you drove seven hundred miles with it. Amazingly, no damage has been done to your transmission. We just replaced the fluid, charged you for the service, and it's fine now. You can pick it up anytime you want."

His disbelief echoed in my ears. "It shouldn't have functioned at all... And I sure don't understand how you drove seven hundred miles." But I knew. I had been clearly assured before I left that I would be protected and that the car would function normally. We humans just do the best we can. God can take care of the rest.

An Angel of Mercy

Kathryn L.M. Reynolds

One September day, more than thirty years ago, I woke up not feeling very well, so my mother kept me home from school. By the afternoon, I was feeling better, so my mother thought nothing more of my illness. The next morning I was again sick, but my mother sent me off to school anyway, understandably thinking I was "sick" because I didn't want to go back to kindergarten class.

At school I can remember one of my classmates attempting to interest me in the playhouse in the back of the classroom, but my head felt woozy and all I wanted to do was rest it on my arms on top of the table where I was sitting. This alarmed my teacher, for normally nothing would have kept me away from that area of the classroom, and she usually had to force me away from it in order to do school work.

I can remember my teacher picking up the black wall phone which was hooked up to the office. I heard her request to speak to my mother. When she got off the phone, she had someone escort me to the nurse's station where I laid down on a cot and waited for my mom to come pick me up.

Mom took me home and had me lie down in bed but by the middle of the afternoon, I was up and running again. My mother says she does not know exactly what it was that made her feel my forehead when I was busy riding my tricycle in the basement, but she did and was alarmed by the heat radiating from my body. My mother immediately made arrangements for my sisters to be picked up from school, and she tucked me into the back seat of her car for the ride to the doctor's office.

The doctor could not understand what was wrong with me. He thought it might be a weird case of the flu and told my mom that I should be watched to see what developed.

To this day, neither the doctor nor my mother understand why he decided to call the hospital to see if I could be admitted, since, besides my high fever, nothing appeared to be wrong with me. On the way to the hospital, I remember lying down in the back seat of our car, watching the power and telephone wires go by with an occasional bird perched on them.

All night long at the hospital, my mom sat by my bedside and she later told me that it was the most frightening experience in her life. She could see me dying before her very eyes, and nobody knew why. While my vital signs weakened by the minute, a surgeon stopped by my room late that night. He picked up my medical chart and then turned to my mom and said, "Ma'am, if I do not immediately operate on your daughter, she is going to die." I was near death from an appendix that had ruptured at least two days before, but I had not shown the usual symptoms of appendicitis. My terrified mom signed the necessary papers. I was placed on a gurney and wheeled toward the operating room. My mother walked beside me as far as she was allowed to go. As they wheeled me into the elevator, I can remember seeing someone standing behind my mother, holding her, as she helplessly watched the doors of the elevator close.

In the operating room, I saw that very same person comforting my mother standing beside me. How reassuring the presence of this person made me feel. I can still remember that comforting voice, telling me not to worry, telling me that I would see my mother in the morning. I recall the black mask being placed over my mouth, and how worried I was because the nurse asked me to try to count backwards and I could barely count forward. Again the same gentle voice spoke to me, telling me not to worry.

While I "slept" on that operating table, I was still in the presence of that same angel who comforted me as I fell asleep. The same one that comforted my mother while she waited and worried.

I "dreamed" of being in an incredibly, indescribable place of beauty, peace and tranquillity. I was in a garden that seemed to be within a garden. Everything was warm and glowing.

There were birds, lots of birds of all different colors. The songs from each bird filled the air with the most beautiful sound as all the bird songs came together and became one glorious harmonious sound. The flowers all had their own special scent, and surprisingly each scent was individual, and instead of being all blended together into an overpowering perfume—I could smell and identify each and every flower's scent.

And all of a sudden I was sitting in a lap that was wonderfully soft and warm with comforting arms wrapped around me. More importantly, I felt safe and warm and comforted. I could *feel* the grass tickling my bare feet, as if it were playing with my toes. My senses became very sharp. I was very much aware of each scent of each flower and the sight and song of each bird. And I felt an enormous sense of comfort and peace.

When I woke up, my mother was standing beside my bed in the recovery room. Just behind her shoulder stood the wonderful person whose voice and presence had so comforted me.

When I pointed this person out to my mother, there was no longer anyone there.

Later, when I asked my mother about the person standing

behind her when I was being wheeled into the operating room, my mom insisted that she had been alone, yet I can clearly remember seeing someone putting loving arms around her. My mom told me that she had not only been all alone, but she'd been praying like mad that I would live. The person standing in the corner of my hospital room with the comforting face and voice, who'd stayed with me throughout the operation was the same person I'd seen comforting my mother as the doors to the operating room closed. The person who had stayed with me throughout the operation had been as real as you or I. It must have been one of God's angels of mercy, perhaps even my guardian angel sent to comfort and help my mother and me through this traumatic experience.

Sometimes a child can see more clearly than an adult, especially when spiritual vision is required.

Inferno

Melinda C. Skaar

For weeks during the spring of 1988, I had been having an odd sense of foreboding—as if something terrible were about to happen in Los Angeles. Strangely, others felt it too. Some thought it might be an earthquake, the Big One. But I dismissed that as silly speculation.

My real concern the night of May 4, 1988, was the special report I was trying to complete for the company president to present to the board of directors. As a new financial analyst with First Interstate Bank of California, I wanted it to be right.

My eyes burned from weariness. I took a moment to turn from the glare of my computer screen to gaze out the window of our thirty-seventh-floor office in downtown L.A. From this height I could see sparkling diamond city lights scattered over the black velvet landscape. It was a far cry from my hometown of Kenyon, Minnesota.

Mom and Dad had visited me two weeks earlier. Mom became anxious looking out the window, wondering how I could work up so high. I shook my head, remembering how concerned they were for my safety in the "big city."

"We're always praying for you, Melinda," said Mom as I kissed her good-bye at the airport. "Oh, Mom," I protested. "You worry about me too much."

"Well, honey," she sighed, looking at me the way she did when I first left home for college, "your father and I can't always be there to help you, but we know the Lord can. Ever since you were a little girl, we've always asked God to cover you with His protection, wherever you are."

I smiled at my reflection in the office window. Here I was, soon to be twenty-nine, with a business degree in finance, making my own way in the world, yet Mom and Dad still thought of me as their little girl. Well, they could pray if they wished; that was their way. But I had been on my own for some time, and you'd think they'd know by now that I had my life pretty well in hand.

A chair scraped on the far side of the office. Stephen Oksas, a tall, thin thirty-one-year-old assistant vice president was also working late.

At 9:45 P.M. I picked up the phone to call my boyfriend. His answering machine clicked on. "Hi, sweetheart," I said, "I expect to finish about ten-thirty. See you soon."

I began putting my papers away at 10:30 P.M., when the phone rang in the outer lobby. I went out to pick it up.

"We believe there is a fire in the building," cautioned a security guard. "Please tell everyone on your floor to leave the building."

I put down the phone and called to Stephen when I was interrupted by the security loudspeaker:

"Attention...attention," crackled the public-address speaker. "We believe there is a fire on the sixteenth floor. Please evacuate the building."

We looked at each other. "Maybe it's just a false alarm and they want to be careful," suggested Stephen. The preceding month we had earthquake drills, learning how to take cover under a desk and then move to the core of the building for protection. But I had never been through a fire drill here. Anyway, with all of the safety systems in the tower, what could go wrong?

The speaker rasped the warning again. "Well," I said with a nervous laugh, "I was leaving anyway."

"I'll get my things," Steve said, then: "Do you smell smoke?"

I did. Overhead I saw black tendrils curling down from open ceiling panels, where workers were about to install a fire-sprinkler system.

Shocked, we hurried to the lobby. Dark fumes seeped through the elevator door cracks. I rushed to one of the stairwells and opened the door. Hot black smoke billowed out. Steve hurried to another stairwell and found the same.

Now I could dimly hear the wail of sirens far below.

Steve and I talked about options: dash down thirty-seven floors through fire, or climb twenty-five stories to the roof? But the stairwells were becoming smoke-filled chimneys. We didn't dare try the elevators. We were trapped.

We groped our way into the nearest office. Steve called security to let them know where we were. The fluorescent ceiling lights began to appear gray behind the gathering smoke. My eyes burned and my nose started to run. I grabbed papers and cardboard and tried to keep the smoke out by blocking the ceiling holes. I stuffed my business-suit jacket under the door, but smoke still seeped in.

We called security again, then the fire department. After a while I decided to call again. This time the telephone line was dead.

The fumes thickened and my throat became parched; I found myself breathing faster to get more oxygen. We needed air. Steve, over six feet tall, picked up a table and smashed it against the window. It bounced off like a basketball.

We tried to hurl an old metal-encased computer, filing cabinet and coat rack against the glass. It was like throwing cardboard boxes at a steel wall.

A piercing roar shook the glass; a helicopter hurtled past outside and hovered a dozen floors above. I grabbed my coat and waved my arms back and forth over my head, thinking that the people in the helicopter must certainly see me.

Stephen tried to pry away the weather striping from the window with sharp, pointed scissors. I joined in. But our attempts to remove the glass were futile. The offices were hot and suffocating. By now, the thick smoke had dulled the lights to grayish black. At least an hour had passed since the security guard had called. Why wasn't anyone coming?

My nose and eyes were streaming from the noxious vapors. Desperate, we retreated to a glass-enclosed copier room that had visibly cleaner air. Once inside, I noticed another door. Pushing it open, we stumbled into a small room neither of us had seen before. It contained a refrigerator, water cooler and floor-to-ceiling storage cabinets.

Grabbing the big empty plastic water bottles, we frantically dug holes in their bottoms with scissors, and stuffed paper towels over the ends as filters. But we could only get a few breaths out of each. We took turns sticking our heads into the cabinets, and then the refrigerator, greedily gulping its icy air. But soon this room, too, filled with smoke.

We lay prostrate, feeling the heat increasing. With my ear to the floor, I could hear the eerie whine of one elevator rising and falling. I became drowsy and fought to remain awake. Steve mumbled, then didn't answer anymore.

I heard a helicopter outside. *If I could get back to the office window, a helicopter pilot might see me,* I thought. Struggling to my knees, I crawled back out into the thick, rolling smoke. The smoke had now filled the office area. Somehow, a certain underlying strength seemed to support me, giving me the will to keep on fighting, to keep on going. As I reached the office window, a helicopter thundered past and flew away. I stood and waved, but all I saw in the smoky glass was a dim reflection of a thin girl with soot-covered face, hand raised weakly, wearing a white blouse that had turned black.

Dizzy, sick, gasping shallow breaths, I slumped in a chair.

"Oh, Dad, Mom," I sighed, "your daughter sure needs help."

I could hear a helicopter in the distance, but it was too far away. I was exhausted and losing hope. It was 3:00 A.M., four-and-a-half-hours since we first smelled smoke. The sounds below seemed to lessen.

I felt completely alone, forgotten and insignificant. My lungs begged for oxygen. I ached from panting. I became very sad, thinking about my family and how they would feel when they got the news, and about the birthday I would never celebrate the coming Sunday.

Then I began to sense that odd strength again. And I knew the reason: Dad and Mom's prayers. I *wasn't* alone. God *was* with me—like a protective covering. I felt an urgency to keep on fighting, to keep on struggling to live.

I blacked out, then came to in a frightening silence. I struggled to focus on reality, fighting to stay alive. Was Steve all right?

Then I saw them...men in dirty yellow coats. I pointed weakly to the little room where Steve lay.

Ripping down draperies to use as stretchers, our rescuers carried us down thirty-seven floors. As they slid me into the ambulance, I glimpsed the dawning sky above and thanked God for being with me.

So many providential things happened that night. Stephen and I survived five-and-a-half-hours in all that smoke. The little refrigerator room had helped keep us alive—a room we had not known was there. Some people will say we were just lucky. I know it was more than that. There was a special support through those five-and-a-half-hours, and it could come only through prayer.

Sunday, May 8, was a special day. It was Mother's Day and my twenty-ninth birthday, and I had recovered enough to call my folks from the hospital. I had to tell them they had given me the greatest gift any parent can give a child. Mom answered the phone.

"Thank you, Mom," I cried. "Thank you and Dad for praying for me. Please don't ever stop."

CHAPTER 2

Give ear to my words, O Lord;

give heed to my sighing.

Listen to the sound of my cry,

my King and my God,

for to you I pray.

O Lord, in the morning you hear my voice;

in the morning I plead my case to you,

and watch.

PSALM 5:1-3 *(NRSV)*

Ways to Pray

Lord, I'm not sure what to pray for.

I believe "all things work for good,"

But I'm sick and confused.

Do I pray for healing?

Do I pray for patience and long-suffering?

If I need to learn, teach me.

If I need to be patient, show me how.

Strengthen my faith, and, if it's Your will,

Heal me.

JANICE K. FEAGIN

Prayer of Relinquishment

Catherine Marshall

Like most people, when I first began active experimentation with prayer, I was full of questions, such as: Why are some agonizingly sincere prayers granted, while others are not?

Today I still have questions. Mysteries about prayer are always ahead of present knowledge—luring, beckoning on to further experimentation.

But one thing I do know; I learned it through hard experience. It's a way of prayer that has resulted consistently in a glorious answer—glorious because each time, power beyond human reckoning has been released. This is the Prayer of Relinquishment.

I got my first glimpse of it in the fall of 1943. I had then been ill for six months with widespread lung infection, and a bevy of specialists seemed unable to help. Persistent prayer, using all the faith I could muster, had resulted in—nothing. I was still in bed full-time.

One afternoon a pamphlet was put in my hands. It was the story of a missionary who had been an invalid for eight years. Constantly she had prayed that God would make her well so that she might do His work. Finally, worn out with futile petition, she prayed, "All right. I give up. If You want me to be an invalid, that's Your business. Anyway, I want You even more than I want health. You decide." In two weeks, the woman was out of bed, completely well.

This made no sense to me, yet I could not forget the story. On the morning of September 14—how can I ever forget the date? —I came to the same point of abject acceptance. "I'm tired of asking," was the burden of my prayer. "I'm beaten through, God. You decide what You want for me."

Tears flowed. I had no faith as I understood faith, expected nothing. The gift of my sick self was made with no trace of graciousness.

And the result? It was as if I had touched a button that opened windows in heaven; as if some dynamo of heavenly power began flowing, flowing. Within a few hours I had experienced the presence of the Living Christ in a way that wiped away all doubt and revolutionized my life. From that moment my recovery began.

Through this incident and others that followed, God was trying to teach me something important about prayer. Gradually, I saw that a demanding spirit, with self-will as its rudder, blocks prayer. I understood that the reason for this is that God absolutely refuses to violate our free will; that, therefore, unless self-will is voluntarily given up, God cannot move to answer prayer.

In time I gained more understanding about the Prayer of Relinquishment through the experiences of others in contemporary life and through books. Jesus' prayer in the Garden of Gethsemane is a pattern for us, I learned. Christ could have avoided the cross. He did not have to go up to Jerusalem that last time. He could have compromised with the priests, bargained with Caiaphas. He could have capitalized on His following and appeased Judas by setting up the beginning of an earthly kingdom. Pilate wanted to release Him, all but begged Him to say the right words—so that he might. Even in the garden on the night of betrayal, He had plenty of time and opportunity to flee, but

Christ used His free will to leave the decision up to His Father.

J. B. Phillips, in his book *The Gospels—Translated Into Modern English* brings Jesus' prayer into focus for us. "Dear Father, all things are possible to You. Please let Me not have to drink this cup. Yet it is not what I want, but what You want."

The prayer was not answered as the human Jesus wished. Yet power has been flowing from His cross ever since.

Even at the moment when Christ was bowing to the possibility of an awful death by crucifixion, He never forgot either the presence or the power of God. The Prayer of Relinquishment must not be interpreted negatively. It does not let us lie down in the dust of a godless universe and steel ourselves just for the worse.

Rather it says: 'This is my situation at the moment. I'll face the reality of it. But I'll also accept willingly whatever a loving Father sends. 'Acceptance therefore never slams the door on hope.'

Yet even with hope our relinquishment must be the real thing, because this giving up of self-will is the hardest thing we human beings are ever called on to do.

I remember the agony of one attractive young girl, Sara, who shared with me her doubts about her engagement. "I love Jeb," she said, "and Jeb loves me. But the problem is, he drinks. Not that he's an alcoholic, you know. Yet the drinking is a sort of symbol of a lot of ideas he has. It has bothered me so much that I wonder if God is trying to tell me to give Jeb up."

As we talked, Sara came to her own conclusion. It was that she would lose something infinitely precious if she did not follow the highest and the best that she knew. Tears glistened in her eyes as she said, "I'm going to break the engagement. If God wants me to marry Jeb, He will see that things change—about the drinking and all."

Right then, simply and poignantly, she told God of her decision. She was putting her broken dreams and her now unknown future into God's hands.

Jeb's ideas and ideals didn't change, so Sara did not marry him. But a year later Sara wrote me an ecstatic letter. "It nearly killed me to give up Jeb. Yet God knew that he wasn't the one for me. Now I've met *the man* and we're to be married. Now *I really* have something to say about trusting God!"

It's good to remember that not even the Master Shepherd can lead if the sheep have not this trust and insist on running ahead of Him or taking side paths or just stubbornly refusing to follow Him. That's the why of Christ's insistence on the practical obedience: "And why call ye Me, Lord, Lord, and do not the things which I say?" (Luke 6:46, *King James Version*). Our pliability must be complete, from our wills right on through to our actions.

When we come right down to it, how can we make obedience real, except as we give over our self-will in reference to each of life's episodes as it unfolds? That's why it shouldn't surprise us that at the heart of the secret of answered prayer lies the Law of Relinquishment.

So Mrs. Nathaniel Hawthorne, wife of the famous American author, found as she wrestled in prayer in the city of Rome one February day in 1860. Una, the Hawthorne's eldest daughter, was dying of a virulent form of malaria. The attending physician, Dr. Franco, had that afternoon warned that unless the young girl's fever abated before morning, she would die.

As Mrs. Hawthorne sat by Una's bed, her thoughts went to what her husband had said earlier that day. "I cannot endure the alternations of hope and fear, therefore I have settled with myself not to hope at all."

But the mother could not share Nathaniel's hopelessness. Una could not, must not, die. This daughter strongly resembled her father, had the finest mind, the most complex character of all the

Hawthorne children. Why should some capricious Providence demand that they give her up?

As the night deepened, the girl lay so still that she seemed to be in the anteroom of death. The mother went to the window and looked out on the piazza. There was no moonlight; a dark and silent sky was heavy with clouds.

*I cannot bear this loss—cannot—cannot...*Then suddenly, unaccountably, another thought took over. *Why should I doubt the goodness of God? Let Him take Una, if He sees best. I can give her to Him. No, I won't fight against Him anymore.*

Then an even stranger thing happened. Having made the great sacrifice, Mrs. Hawthorne expected to feel sadder. Instead she felt lighter, happier than at any time since Una's long illness had begun

Some minutes later, she walked back to the girl's bedside, felt her daughter's forehead. It was moist and cool. Una was sleeping naturally. And the mother rushed into the next room to tell her husband that a miracle had happened.

Now the intriguing question is: What is the spiritual law implicit in this Prayer of Relinquishment?

Fear is like a screen erected between us and God, so that His power cannot get through to us. So, how does one get rid of fear?

This is not easy when the life of someone dear hangs in the balance, or when what we want most is involved. At such time, every emotion, every passion, is tied up in the dread that what we fear most is about to come upon us. Obviously only drastic measures can deal with such a gigantic fear and the demanding spirit that usually goes along with it. My experience has been that trying to deal with it by repeating faith affirmations is not drastic enough.

So then we are squarely up against the Law of Relinquishment. Was Jesus showing us how to use this law when

He said, "resist not evil" (Matthew 5:39)? In God's eyes, fear is evil because it's an acting out of lack of trust in Him. So Jesus is advising: Resist not fear. (Note that He made only one exception to this: "Fear him [the Devil] which is able to destroy both soul and body in hell" [Matthew 10:28].)

In other words, Jesus is saying, admit the possibility of what you fear most. And lo, as you stop fleeing, force yourself to walk up to the fear, look it full in the face—never forgetting that God and His power are still the supreme reality—the fear evaporates. Drastic? Yes. But it is one sure way of releasing prayer power into human affairs.

God Takes Our Burdens

Van Varner

Elizabeth, Elizabeth, what happened!

You were an original, unique, there was no one like you, and now, at age eighty-one, you're a recluse, not having left your bed for six years. Only three people see you: the loyal woman who comes in once a day to clean and fix the small amount of food you eat; your son, my godson, who visits from California, and I. The other men and women who were close to you have all died. You have defied all attempts to let a doctor visit; all those plans to go to the West Coast you've canceled.

I see you only occasionally now, but I telephone you, or you phone me, once or twice or three times a day. You'll say, "I want to know how you are feeling," and I'll say, "I'm fine, how are you?" and you'll reply, "fine," and I'll conclude, "Then that makes two of us."

I am resigned. I am resigned in all areas save one. Those efforts to bring God to your room have been tactfully deflected; but do you know what? There is hope. There is hope because I have been praying for you these many years, and I shall go on praying, and others who read this will, I dare say, pray for you, and you shall see the benefits.

When? In God's time. In God's time.

That One Thing I Could Do

Ernestine Scott

"Mrs. Scott? This is the police. We have your son Charles."

Thirteen-year-old Charles? My Charles? "What has he done?" I asked, my voice shaking.

"We'd rather talk to you here," the officer said. "Can you come down now?"

My heart was pounding as I drove through the streets of our small town. My husband, Charles's father, had died only a month earlier after a short battle with cancer; the four children and I were barely beginning to cope with that unspeakable loss.

And now my oldest son was in trouble with the law! It couldn't be true. My husband and I had taught our children right from wrong; our lives revolved around our church and its activities. Charles was mischievous, but he wasn't a "bad" boy. There had to be some mistake.

My knees shook as I walked into a police station for the first time in my life. Charles was sitting there, pale with fright, looking completely out of place in cutoff jeans, a torn shirt and bare feet. A friend of Charles stood nearby, shifting nervously from foot to foot.

"They shot at a window of a parked car with a BB gun," a police officer told me. "I've explained the seriousness of the situation to them, and I hope the boys can pay for the damage out of their allowances."

We worked things out, and Charles seemed suitably sorry. On the way home, I prayed this would be the last sign of reckless behavior in the son I'd asked to be "man of the house," now that his daddy was gone.

A year and a half later, I met and married Bob Scott, a wonderful man with two children of his own. Charles liked and accepted his stepfather, but by this time, Charles was a teenager giving us all kinds of new problems.

He had good grades, but he cut classes and sometimes skipped school altogether. Even though he was a good athlete, he refused to join any school teams; instead he hung out with friends we didn't approve of. He ignored his assigned chores at home and violated his curfew. He didn't show up at his afternoon school job. And then came the shattering realization that he and some of his friends were using drugs.

"He's throwing his life away," I cried to Bob. We tried to discipline Charles in every way we could think of. We asked for help from his Scout leaders, his teachers and counselors, and our minister. We met with a psychologist. I even saw a psychiatrist.

Nothing seemed to make an impression on him.

Three months before graduation, Charles came to me with an announcement. "Mom," he said, "I'm quitting school."

I cried, cajoled, threatened, begged him to consider what this would do to his future. Nothing worked. He didn't care.

In desperation, Bob and I told him he'd have to get a job or join the military service. Charles chose the navy, and on a gray spring day, we hugged him hard and put him on a bus for basic training in California.

Letters from Charles came in spurts, on again, off again. He was being trained as a clerk, he told us. At last I thought he'd found his own "place" and work he could commit himself to! But when letters arrived saying he hated the discipline of military life, I wrote back as quickly and as often as I could. "I'm praying for you," I told him.

Charles was assigned to serve on an aircraft carrier, and his discontent erupted again. "I can't stand the navy," he wrote. "I'm going AWOL."

I couldn't believe his words. I lay awake all night, twisting with frustration and concern. I wrote letter after letter telling him what the consequences of desertion would be. "I'm praying for you," I told him again.

I *was* praying for him, in my own fashion. During this painful time, it happened that a friend called and asked me to join a prayer group. At first I hesitated. I'd always been a churchgoer; I'd always said my prayers. It just didn't seem necessary to join a prayer group. But I did join, and gradually I began to see how my prayers had been pretty shallow. About this time I came across a little booklet that was to change my life. It contained a list of scriptural references grouped together in what is called "The Prayer of Committal" (see page 62). As the booklet explained, it is a "commonsense kind of prayer" that is "summarized in three phases: 'Commit, trust and He worketh.'"

If I was wakened by worry during the night, when I opened my eyes first thing in the morning, and as I went about my daily tasks, I repeated those verses to myself and made them the basis of my prayers about my son. I was learning something about what the Apostle Paul called prayer without ceasing.

Now when Charles's letters arrived, roiling with discontent and full of threats, I took a deep breath and repeated "The Prayer of Committal." Instead of panicking and allowing my fears about Charles to accelerate into a paralyzing spiral, I repeated those verses.

Throughout the day, throughout letter after troubled letter, I repeated quietly to myself again and again: *Commit everything you do to the Lord... You can move mountains if you believe.* As I repeated these solid, specific promises, they became rock that made my faith stronger every day. They enabled me to "let go" of my despair—and give Charles to the Lord, trustingly.

Each time one of his letters arrived that upset me, I turned to my Bible. Pray and believe... Commit your way to the Lord; trust in Him and He will act.

Charles didn't go AWOL. The Vietnam War was now winding down, and Charles was sent home a year early with an honorable discharge.

I threw my arms around him, my world-weary "old man" of twenty years. He was home safe, but he never smiled. He tried job after job, project after project. There was a succession of false starts and many disappointments as he told us his employers "didn't appreciate" him or the work "wasn't right" for him. He seemed so lost, and my old panic for him started to come back.

No, I wouldn't allow it! I clung to the "Prayer of Committal:" *Trust in Him and He will act... We have the Holy Spirit through faith.* Pray. Pray without ceasing.

At last Charles had a job that seemed to be working out. He moved to a nearby town and we breathed a sigh of relief.

And then came the call from his boss. Charles was in serious trouble and being arraigned before a judge that very day. My husband and I rushed to the courthouse, praying all the way. When we found Charles, he's already gone before the judge and been given probation. "I think I've hit bottom," he said. But for the first time he sounded like a man who knew the only way now was up.

We respected his wish to keep his problems a secret, especially from the rest of the family. His probation officer arranged for him to get another job, and this time he put his all into it.

Then arose what looked like a new problem: One of Charles's

old friends appeared; he and Charles had been involved in the drug scene years before. I flushed with anger when I first saw him sitting there talking with Charles. But my anger turned to astonishment. They had Bibles open in their laps, and were deep in discussion. This young man had sought out Charles to tell him about his new life as a Christian.

From then on, Charles read his Bible daily and became a serious student of its words. He talked to me about Scriptures, and chose a little church, which he attended regularly.

At first, it was hard for us to believe Charles's transformation was permanent. But instead of his interest diminishing, it increased. As months, then a year went by, Charles not only settled down and progressed in his job, but he also started helping others who were down-and-out, giving them a hand and leading them in Bible study. My lost boy was really home! He blossomed with a sincere, sweet boldness that was apparent to everyone. I had committed; I had trusted, and He had, as it says in Psalm 37:4, given me the desires of my heart.

What can I say to all the parents whose hearts are heavy with worry for sons and daughters gone astray?

Release your child to the Lord. Commit your prayers to God.

And pray. Pray without ceasing.

THE PRAYER OF COMMITTAL:

These are the scriptures involved in the prayer. I've only used phrases to identify them, because I think it's important for the person who uses them to look them up and copy the full text.

PSALM	37:5	*"Commit thy way unto the Lord...."*
PSALM	57:1	*"My soul trusteth in thee...."*
MATTHEW	17:20	*"...Faith as a grain of mustard seed...."*
MARK	11:24	*"When ye pray, believe...."*

ACTS	2:39	*"For the promise is...to your children...."*
ACTS	16:31	*"Thou shalt be saved, and thy house."*
ROMANS	4:20	*"...Strong in faith, giving glory to God."*
GALATIANS	3:14	*"Receive the promise of the Spirit through faith."*
PHILIPPIANS	4:19	*"My God shall supply all your need...."*
HEBREWS	4:3	*"For we which have believed do enter into rest...."*
HEBREWS	11:1	*"...Evidence of things not seen."*
I JOHN	5:14	*"He heareth us" (I added this one myself.)*

Out of My Control

Bradlee E. Webber

Numb with worry, I sped down the freeway toward the hospital where rescue units had taken my three kids. "I was afraid that trip was a mistake from the beginning," I exploded to my wife, Kim. "That's a twenty-one hour drive each way." I let off steam so I wouldn't have to think about how badly hurt the kids might be. The camper had lost a wheel and flipped on the freeway, just one-half hour short of home.

I had tried to tell my ex-wife, Debbie, the trip wasn't a good idea. But since the divorce I didn't have anything to say about what happened to the kids. I had to depend on Debbie to make responsible decisions, and this was what she had decided. She, her sister and their mother were driving our three kids and their two cousins from Portland to Disneyland and back, and there wasn't a thing I could do about it. Now, my worst fears had come to pass. Not only did I not have control, I might have lost them altogether.

At the hospital, we found my eight-year-old son, Aaron, in the emergency room, surrounded by doctors who worked to keep him breathing. His face was bloody and swollen and he had a breathing tube in his mouth.

"Aaron, it's Dad. Can you hear me?" I took hold of his hand.

"You are going to be okay. The doctors will fix you up. Do you understand?" He squeezed my hand. "I'll be here when you wake up. I love you," I said, and the orderlies wheeled him away to surgery. I felt helpless. I had to trust that they were the best surgeons available.

The nurse told me that Jason, my sixteen-year-old, had suffered only minor bumps and bruises, and my ex-wife had been admitted. But meanwhile, five-year-old Jesseca was in the intensive care unit. The doctor there told us a CAT scan revealed a bad concussion. The pressure on her brain could be fatal, and they were considering a skull tap to relieve it. I felt sick; this was a nightmare.

After three hours in intensive care, I needed to go and check on Aaron. Jesse begged me not to go. I stayed with her until she fell asleep around 10:00 P.M. The nurse told us that Jesse would be woken up every half-hour so she wouldn't slip into a coma. "You go to Aaron and I'll stay with her," Kim said.

I let my mom know what was happening, then I dialed my good friend Mike Teeters. Mike and I had worked together as mechanics for TRI-MET, the bus system here in Portland. He had got me interested in searching the Scriptures for answers to life's problems. I needed to talk to him now. I told him what had happened and said, "Will you pray for them?"

"I'll meet you there," Mike said. Alone now for a few minutes, I wrestled with my faith. How could God let this happen? I felt angry at Him. I wanted my kids to live, to be perfect again. That was my will. But I knew it was out of my control. What was God's will?

I knew that sometimes God says no. Some children die, even though the parents pray as hard as they can. Who was I to expect any special favors from God? I tried to prepare myself to accept His will, if it should be different from mine.

Soon Mike came through the door and hugged me. I told him that Aaron was still in surgery after five-and-a-half hours. Together we walked to a vast lobby, where Kim's parents were waiting. Kim's mother said she had phoned their church's prayer chain.

"I think we should pray now," Mike said. We formed a circle and held hands. Then we took turns praying aloud. We acknowledged God's presence—where two or more are gathered in His name, as the Bible says. Someone asked God to comfort me, and I did feel comforted. We prayed for the doctors' wisdom, their skills, their hands, and most of all we prayed for Aaron and Jesseca to be restored to health. Mike wrapped it up by saying, "We surrender the children to Your loving care, Lord. They're in Your hands."

I felt encouraged. If God wouldn't listen to me, surely He would listen to these people who seemed closer to Him. When my own faith faltered, I hung on to theirs. I began to allow myself to count on Him to come through for me.

The surgeons, dressed in pale green with tight-fitting green caps, came from the operating room. White surgical masks hung from their necks. We shook hands and they sat down across from us at a low round table. "We feel pleased that we've been able to pretty well reconstruct his face," one surgeon said. He went on to explain in detail how they had handled each of the broken bones in Aaron's face. He said Aaron would temporarily be unable to speak because of the tracheotomy.

"Will he look the same?" Kim's mother asked the question I had been afraid to ask. Everyone had always said he looked like me.

"There's no way to predict. Really, I think he'll look normal once the swelling goes down, but no, he won't look *exactly* the same as he did. There's just no way. Remember, he is very lucky to be alive."

I stood up and shook the doctors' hands. I'd heard enough. "Thank you, doctors. I appreciate it," I said. "I know you've done your best."

I heard the words, the polite phrases, but I felt anger rising up again. Yes, thank God he's alive, but he'll never look the same. Never *be* the same. Sure, it could have been worse—but it also could have been better. It could have not happened at all! I had to force myself to focus on my gratitude to God for sparing Aaron's life.

But I felt like screaming at Debbie. Why hadn't she listened to me? Deep down I knew it wasn't all her fault. I struggled to control my feelings.

Next I was blaming myself. Since the divorce I'd had no control. A father should be able to keep things like this from happening and I hadn't. I fought to keep from breaking down as I went upstairs to be with Aaron when he woke up. I had promised him. I could control that. Aaron's face was still swollen and he was breathing through a tube. I knew he hurt; a single tear trickled down his cheek. He pointed to his mouth, and I gave him a sip of water. Then I stayed the rest of the night with him. By 5:00 A.M. I was dead tired, but I wanted to check on Jesse. Aaron tried to hold on to my hand, tried to keep me from leaving. I assured him I'd be right back. When I reached Jesse, they had taken a second CAT scan. The hemorrhaging had stopped, and the mass of fluid in her skull had dissipated! The doctor said that almost never happens with such a large mass, adding, "I don't know where it went, but it's gone. She's laughing!" The nurse said it was amazing to view the two scans. "You wouldn't believe it was the same little girl!" But I believed it; after all, there were at least four prayer chains going. I knew God had heard us.

When I returned to Aaron, I took a marker board and pen so that he could communicate with me. I also took along some pictures of him in his Little League uniform. I wanted him to imagine himself well and playing ball again. The first things Aaron wrote on his board were "Where's Mom?" and "How is Jesse?" Of course! In my anxiety about protecting him from any news that would worry him, I had neglected to let him know that everyone was alive. I was grateful that all the news was relatively good. He was the worst injured of the group. After they released Jesseca, we were told Aaron would have to undergo more surgery to remove some packing and to put in a smaller breathing tube. He looked scared when I told him, but I explained that he might be able to talk after the operation. The new tube would be small enough that he could cover the opening and get air up through his throat.

The next morning I waited in a small, semi-darkened family area near the operating room. His mother was still hospitalized. I would see him through this. It hurt to send him back into surgery after what he'd already been through. I paced like a caged animal for an hour and a half.

"Mr. Webber?" The surgeon appeared in the doorway. "The operation went well. Aaron would like to see you."

I stepped into the hall just as they pushed Aaron out through the double doors of surgery. I bent over the gurney and ran my fingers through his straight blond hair, just the way I used to do to put him to sleep when he was a baby.

"How ya doin', little buddy?" He covered the opening in the tube with his small fingers. "I can talk now," he croaked, smiling as best he could. Then he whispered, "I love you, Dad."

To hear him speak at all was music to my ears, but to have that be the first thing he wanted to say was more than I could handle. I just lost it. I let go and cried.

And in that moment, all the anger, all the frustration simply disappeared. *Thank You, Lord,* I prayed, *thank You.*

I saw now that I really didn't have to be in control of my kids. They were in His hands, as Mike had said. Where I was powerless, God was powerful. I had to turn it all over to Him. I had no choice. Anger wasn't doing me any good and it certainly wasn't helping the kids.

As I let go of the anger I felt more open to God's will than ever before. Silently I asked Him what He wanted me to do, how I could help my kids. The answer, I thought I heard Him say, was, *Just love, them, no matter what.*

The accident brought things into focus for me. At the time when the kids needed me most, the only thing I had to give them was love. And that's the way it will have to be from now on. My discipline over my kids and most of my time with them are gone. But I'll always have the power to love them. Love is the most powerful force of all. And that is certainly in my control.

Yelling at God

Rhoda Blecker

There was a long period in my life when I lived rationally, in my head and body rather than in my faith and soul. Then something happened that defied rational explanation. In mid December of 1971, I awoke one morning with the vivid recollection of a dream. It was unusual for me to remember any dream, but this one was haunting. My face turned dark blue, and doctors said they could not treat me. They advised I seek help across the country at a place in Connecticut, a monastery where nuns lived. They told me its name and sent me away.

At scattered moments during my workday, the memory of the dream returned more urgently each time. Finally I closed my office door, dialed the Connecticut area code and brusquely asked the directory assistance operator if she had a listing for a monastery by the name I had been given in my dream. *This will settle it,* I thought.

She gave me the number.

I must have sat at my desk for an hour, staring at the phone and feeling stunned. Around 4:15 P.M., I finally dialed the number. When someone answered, I asked only, "If I were to send a contribution, to whom would I direct it?" The person on the other end gave me a name and address. I thanked her. I wrote a check and sent it off with a letter that read, in its entirety, "I do not know who you are. Here is a contribution. I am Jewish." And I signed it. I did not explain that for me being Jewish didn't mean I was observant. I wasn't. To me, Judaism meant no more than social action.

Afterward, I decided I must have read the name of the monastery somewhere and it had stuck in my subconscious like a splinter, drawn out only in the free association of the dream state. Then a letter arrived from one of the nuns, Mother Miriam. She thanked me for my contribution and told me about her monastic order, which was dedicated to prayer and work, according to the Rule of Saint Benedict. She asked, "Miss Blecker, have you thought about why you wrote to us?"

I replied in a return letter, somewhat tentative, "I seem to feel that social action isn't enough."

By the time she responded it was early January. She sent me two books by Abraham Joshua Heschel, a twentieth-century Jewish theologian. As I held the books, a shiver went down my back. The supervisor on my first job was Heschel's niece. I had been introduced to him at her wedding. *Get a grip,* I told myself. *It's just a coincidence.*

My firm practice on work nights was to go to bed after the eleven o'clock news, but that night I stayed awake reading one of the Heschel books. Sometime around 1:00 A.M. I smelled smoke. I ran into the kitchen and saw fire erupting on my service porch, where the gas water-heater and a utility sink were located. Frantically I filled and dumped a pot of water again and again until I doused the flames. Later, the investigators from the gas company told me, "The place could have gone up in a flash if you hadn't acted so quickly."

What if I hadn't stayed up late reading a book I had received that very day from Mother Miriam? Another coincidence? I wasn't sure anymore, but I thought that I should thank Mother Miriam anyway.

The most severe blizzards in decades had struck Connecticut that year and on a whim, I decided to send some birdseed because there might be birds on the grounds who found it hard going. I bought twenty pounds of birdseed and shipped it off with a note reading. "Thank you for the books. If you have any winter birds at the convent, please give them a meal on me."

The letter I received from Mother Miriam read, "Now I believe you have been connected to us for some purpose." It seemed Mother Miriam in fact fed the birds each and every morning and had run out of birdseed the day before my package arrived. The 200 pounds she had ordered had not been delivered because of the snow, and she feared she would have to turn the birds away hungry for the first time in seventeen years. That day the mail arrived with the birdseed I had sent, exactly ten percent of what she had ordered and just enough to tide her over until the shipment arrived.

It was then I was sure something was going on.

I was single at the time, miserably lonely, a workaholic. More than anything, I thought, I wanted a man in my life, a partner. Knowing that Mother Miriam was praying for me, I started trying to pray on my own. But my prayers took a different form than I had imagined.

I began sitting in the front window of my second-floor apartment late at night, looking out over the deserted street and *yelling* at God. It was the best I could manage at the time. I didn't worry about such considerations as awe or fear, and I certainly didn't count my blessings. I told God that if I was really in his thoughts, the way Mother Miriam said I was, he ought to be able to see I needed someone. He ought to bring that person to me, someone who shared my interests and background, the kind of man I had been looking for with the kind of specifications I had carefully constructed in my mind. I had spent ten years dating and it had led me nowhere but the windowsill.

I didn't tell Mother Miriam that I was yelling at God. Six months after I began yelling, I met the man I married. Keith and I found each other in a little neighborhood coffee shop where I ate breakfast every day. Honestly, I couldn't have done better if I had picked him out myself, but I know I didn't, because I never would have chosen him. Keith was anything but the man of my dreams. I fancied myself an intellectual; he was a laborer. I was a member of a profession; he owned a small pool-cleaning service. There was no way we could have ever gotten together without God being our matchmaker. That was the *only* explanation my mind could accept.

And Keith told me something interesting; He too had started sitting up at night yelling at God, right before he began eating breakfast at the coffee shop.

Like me, my husband was searching. His youthful experience with religion had been fraught with ambivalence, and as a result, Keith had never had any formal beliefs. After our marriage, he remained aloof from Mother Miriam, thinking the nuns might try to convert him. "You don't know these nuns," I said.

Early in our friendship I had asked Mother Miriam, "Will we reach a point when the only way for us to continue would be for me to become a Catholic. Because I can't."

Mother Miriam had replied patiently, "You and I are friends no matter what. But I'd like you to think about something. You are a Jewish woman, and you don't know what that means, not really. Why don't you try to find out?"

In 1981, ten years after I had my dream, Keith and I visited the monastery during the Christmas season. When I met Mother Miriam at last, we threw our arms around each other and hugged as if we were soul mates (which we were, in a true sense). I helped set up the crèche and carried hay in from the barn to lay around the manger. A priest looked on with pleasure and said to me, "Thank you so much for bringing Christmas."

For a moment I was uncomfortable. Then it occurred to me: If it hadn't been for a Jewish woman, there wouldn't be Christmas. "You're welcome, Father," I said quietly.

Later in the visit the oldest nun, well into her eighties, took my hands after Christmas Mass. "You don't know what a gift you give us by being here at this time. When Reverend Mother sings the genealogy of Jesus before midnight Mass, every name she's singing is a Jewish name. You are a sign to us of continuity and truth."

I related all this to Mother Miriam, who once again suggested I look more deeply into my Judaism. Several weeks later, back home in Los Angeles, I was flipping through the television channels on Sunday morning and came upon someone saying, "The problem is that Jews don't pray in the synagogue." That caught my attention, and I watched the rest of the program. At the end the speaker was identified as a Los Angeles rabbi. His congregation happened to be within walking distance from my house.

So I met the rabbi and found myself talking to him about needing something more in my life and not knowing where to find it. I did not tell him I had been sent by a nun.

Keith and I were childless. My husband and I were strongly dependent upon each other. I knew if something happened to one of us, the other would be badly adrift. We needed something more than just each other to embrace.

I proposed to Keith that I reexplore my Jewish spiritual roots. He was fine with that, and he accompanied me to services. On the eve of Yom Kippur in 1985, the rabbi spoke about how lonely it was to be an observant Jew in the modern world. The theme of loneliness struck a chord with Keith. For many years, like me, he had struggled with spiritual loneliness. He asked the rabbi if he could attend his classes. I felt an amazing sense of pride when my husband, who had a GED, began to study Hebrew. Three quarters of the way through the class, he told me he wanted to become a practicing Jew.

Mother Miriam was ecstatic. She believed that a life with faith is infinitely better than a life without faith. It was a discovery I had made for myself, with Mother Miriam's gentle urgings, when I moved beyond the rationality that had been a barrier to the richness of the soul. Spiritual loneliness is the greatest ache of all, and the absence in my life of a loving relationship with God at its center had been the greatest loneliness I could ever know.

How, I find myself asking, did I get here from where I started? When I say, "I was lucky," the rabbi nods, and the priest shakes his head and corrects me, "You were blessed." When I ask, "Why me?" the rabbi shrugs, and Mother Miriam says, "Why not you?"

In hundreds of small ways, my experience with Mother Miriam and the nuns is wrapped up in the most incredible happenstance. But I am no longer surprised by what some people call "coincidences." To me, coincidence often denotes a point where the divine intersects with our earthbound lives.

This is the journey I have made, pushed, I am convinced, by more than mere chance. I have learned to say prayers of thanks and prayers of praise, and I don't yell at God any longer. I did not come back because I believed in the miracles of the Bible and my tradition, but because I had been brought, after all, to believe there are such things as miracles. All we have to do is recognize those miracles when they happen.

As a rational person, I know I can prove nothing; but the fact is I no longer feel a need to. I am far happier and fulfilled now than when my story began.

Extraordinary Meeting

Edward A. Elliot

It meant a day out of our vacation, but my wife and I strongly felt that we should make the effort while we were in Maine to go see Dr. Reuben Larson, an eighty-year-old missionary pioneer. After lunch during our visit, quite out of the blue, Dr. Larson asked, "Ed, in all your travels have you ever run into an Indian named Bakht Singh?"

How extraordinary! Only two weeks before, on one of his infrequent visits to the United States, Bakht Singh had invited me to lunch. I told Dr. Larson what I'd learned about Singh, how he was one of India's best-known Christian leaders, how he had founded hundreds of churches and had preached to thousands. Whenever he traveled, believers gathered at train stations to speak and pray with him for just a few minutes.

The things I told about this godly man had a strange effect on Dr. Larson. He was literally openmouthed. Finally he explained why.

"Many years ago in western Canada, I met a young Indian engineering student who was interested in the Christian faith. His name was Bakht Singh. For fifty years I've been praying for him, praying that he would come to know God better and serve Him. I've always wondered what became of him."

It wasn't long after our visit that Dr. Larson died. But even before then I knew why we'd taken that day out of our vacation to see him. We were meant to bring him the news that he had waited fifty years to hear.

Conversational Prayer

Phil Bowner

I was nervous that day back in 1976 when, as a young attorney, I prepared to try my first case as a new Christian. As I stood amid the noise and confusion of the Fulton County Courthouse in Atlanta, Georgia, while the courtroom was being made ready, I wanted nothing so much as to find an empty room or quiet corner where I could pray. But there was none. It seemed as though every nook and cranny of the courthouse was jammed with people.

Then, down a hall I spotted a line of telephone booths, one of them empty. I squeezed into it, and as I began to pray, I found that quite unaware, I had lifted the receiver to my ear. "Lord," I said, "You know I'm new at this. Help me do a good job for my client. But most important, let me serve You in this work." It didn't take more than a minute. When I hung up the receiver I felt calm and confident too.

"Call unto Me, and I will answer thee..." God promised us in Jeremiah 33:3. Indeed, He does. And I wasn't even expected to drop a coin for the call.

God's Chat Line

Janet Russell

We moved to a new area two years ago. I joined a small local church and became involved in a ladies growth group. The ladies in the group were six wonderful, busy younger moms. I felt happy to be part of the group, but sadly, none of these ladies had the time to begin a new friendship with this young grandma.

I knew how to be a friend and I knew how to reach out and to be patient. After months of aloneness, I remembered that my friend, Jesus, was just waiting to share one of His friends with me. I had asked for a friend who would chat about grown children, husbands, aging, someone who enjoyed similar hobbies, but most of all, I asked for a prayer partner.

An exciting idea came to mind. I had a new computer and enjoyed spending a couple of hours each day surfing the Internet so why not search for an online chat partner? I mentioned the idea to my husband and oldest daughter and their looks of concern and cautioning remarks almost discouraged me completely.

But being a discerning grandma, I logged on and met one. I bypassed two, three, and four. I carefully chatted with this new friend, who liked quilting, fishing, and reading, and we gradually got to know each other like 'pen pals.'

We chatted about her granddaughter who lives ten hours away

from her and the sixteen feet of snow each winter in her town in northern Canada. After a week of chatting, I confided in her that I had been feeling isolated in my new surroundings and found myself telling her about my plans to seek out newcomers at our church and invite them for Sunday breakfast, so that they would find companionship. I held my breath when she replied, "What church do you belong to?" When I answered, we discovered that we were members of the same denomination, and my new friend replied, "We're sisters." She went on to tell me that her prayer partner and friend was extremely worried about her involvement with this chat line, so she couldn't wait to share the good news about our friendship.

Now, we chat once or twice a week and pray for each other and our families.

God did not give us a spirit of fear but of love and of power and of a sound mind. Wherever I am, or have been, or will go, God is with me; His love surrounds me, and He blesses me. What a friend!

How to Pray for Your Daughter

Polly Wolf

As a mother of five children, I have had many answered prayers.

When my children were small, their father spent two tours in Vietnam and I lived on prayer strength.

My youngest was a submissive child, with a great desire to please me. At the age of seventeen, she met a young man and her submissiveness and desire to please changed from me to him.

He was a very controlling, self-centered person, and took control of her mind, her emotions, and soon became very verbally, emotionally, and physically abusive.

I cried out unto the Lord, praying every way I knew how for the Lord to open her eyes. Finally, I simply said, "Lord Jesus, I do not know how to pray for her anymore, and I know you are no respecter of persons—you love the soul of that boy as well as you love her. Together they are destroying each other, but I am responsible for her. Please, somehow, show me what to do and how to pray."

A couple of days later, I was in a Christian bookstore and was looking through the book shelves when I came across a book, *How to Pray for Your Daughter*. I opened it up and the first thought was "I don't believe in 'canned prayers.'" But the Holy

Spirit reminded me that I had asked for a way to pray, so I bought the book and took it home.

My daughter had been gone all day with her boyfriend. When she didn't come home at the expected time, I stopped everything and began to pray in earnest. At 2:00 A.M., after praying and weeping until there was nothing left, I reached for the book I had bought on prayer. The author had taken actual Bible verses dealing with various subjects and inserted the words, "my daughter" into them making them very personal. There was an index where I could choose a prayer subject, such as "fear" or "confusion."

At first, I began to simply repeat the words as I read them. Then the Spirit began to cut deep into my heart and I was near to God and I knew it. My heart began to fill with strength as I claimed God's precious word on her behalf.

God honored the many hours of prayer—placing my daughter's name in His Word. Today, my daughter is free from that boy and married to one who cherishes her. They are serving the Lord faithfully.

Mothers—Don't ever stop praying for your teens, or claiming God's power through His Word!

The Prayer
of Agreement

Anonymous

In July, after I had been married for twenty-seven years, my wife confessed to me that she had been involved with a man that worked for me for two years. She told me it was over. I told her I loved her and wanted to save our marriage.

In September, she moved out while I was traveling on business, without telling me where she had gone. She left a note telling me that she did not love me anymore and never wanted to see me again. She said we had grown apart and that she did not feel that I loved her anymore.

In October, she filed for divorce. She had a friend of hers call me and say that her lawyer had advised against talking to me for any reason.

I talked with a pastor I knew and respected, seeking advice. He listened to me, then told me that in his estimation, my marriage was over and that I should accept it and move on. He also advised that I do everything possible to protect myself legally. I was stunned. Almost without exception, my friends and relatives told me the same thing. I was left, it seemed, with no hope. Thank God I had a few Christian friends who said that as long as God still answers prayers, there is always hope, and that they were praying for me.

I talked with my lawyer. He advised that I should file for divorce immediately and do everything possible to protect myself, even it if hurt my wife. I told him I was not ready to do that. I wanted to talk with some friends for advice first.

It seemed things were spinning out of control and my life was coming apart at the seams. I was being shunned by friends that I had known for years based on lies being spread by the wife I loved. My children turned against me. I was locked out of my house. I was even sent to jail, based on lies.

The truth came out weeks later, but by that time, the damage had been done. I was amazed at how fast friends and even relatives will turn on you when they think they may gain something from your divorce. My lawyer told me that divorce and death will bring out the very worst in people. He told me I would be better by the time my divorce was final.

I was looking for anything to give me hope. When I am worried or afraid and I do not know which way to turn or what to do, I read the Psalms and I pray. I prayed as I hadn't for years. I constantly prayed my heart out to God. I read I Corinthians, chapter thirteen about love.

I called my lawyer back and told him that I could not do anything to harm someone I loved. I also told him I wanted him to do everything he could to delay the divorce.

I wrote my wife a letter and told her I would never agree to a divorce. The judge could sign the divorce decree, but I never would.

I decided to do everything I possibly could to save my marriage. I sent my wife letters telling her how much I loved her and how much she meant to me. I told her I wanted her to come home so we could start to rebuild our lives.

But most importantly, I prayed for my wife.

I finally did find a Christian counselor I trusted. He told me I had to put my life into God's hands and trust His will for my life. He told me that the most important thing for my wife and me was to seek God's will, then, be willing to trust God's will for my life.

We prayed a prayer he called 'A Prayer of Agreement,' which he explained as two Christians agreeing on a thing that they know clearly is God's will and then praying for it. He said we would pray that God would remove any delusions that my wife was operating under, and that she would understand God's will for her life.

I was finally able to trust my fate to God's love, no matter what the outcome.

Several weeks later my wife called me at work. While she was sleeping one night, she had a dream that opened her eyes. It was like coming out of a bad dream. She wanted to meet me to see if there was a chance for us.

Well, to make a long and painful story shorter, I can tell you that we are back together. My wife has rediscovered a faith in God.

I have been told by marriage counselors that ninety-nine percent of the marriages that get to the point of break-up end in divorce. God had other plans.

While You Wait

Mathew Woodley

After seven years of faithful ministry in a small-town church, I knew that God was calling my family into a new venture. Unfortunately, He wasn't in a hurry to tell us where. One chapter in our lives was ending, but as far as we could tell, God hadn't even written the first sentence of the next. So for two years we waited...and waited...and waited for God to do something, say something, lead us *somewhere.*

Of course, I did my best to *make* things happen. I diligently pursued six promising options. God shut every door. Disappointed and angry, I pleaded with God, "Lord, what are You doing? Am I going to stand still forever?" After haggling with God, I started arguing with my wife. *After all,* I thought, *this waiting business has to be somebody's fault.* I was beyond impatient. I felt abandoned and useless.

During this two-year holding pattern, I kept bumping against the Bible's frequent advice to "wait for the Lord" and began to think more deeply about this process. How do we wait for God? What does it look like? It's an understatement to say that we live in a culture of the quick fix (even in the church). Tools, books, formulas, and programs incessantly promise to clear our arteries overnight, resolve marital conflict, tighten flabby stomachs, lift depression, and bestow instant intimacy with God. Clearly, waiting is difficult and countercultural.

But if we change our perspective a bit, we can begin to see waiting as a gift from God instead of a burden. Jeremiah wrote, "It is good to wait quietly for the salvation of the LORD" (Lamentations 3:26). Waiting is not only necessary; it's good. Those who wait for God experience His salvation in times of trouble (Isaiah 33:2). Waiting on God renews our strength so that we can "soar on wings like eagles" (Isaiah 40:31). Obedient waiting is the pathway to inheriting God's blessings (Psalm 37:34). Waiting is intimately linked with answered prayer (Psalm 38:15, Micah 7:7). Finally, Isaiah promised, "No ear has perceived, no eye has seen any God besides you, who acts on behalf of those who wait for him" (Isaiah 64:4).

In the midst of our instant gratification culture, how should we respond when God isn't in a hurry? After reflecting on Scripture and my own experience, I've identified five stages in the waiting process. This is not a formula. Rather, each stage represents one leg of a journey, a journey toward maturity that sometimes seems slow and painful. But as Jesus leads us through these phases of spiritual growth, He will produce a rich harvest within and through our lives (James 5:7).

FIGHTING

I hate to wait. Let's face it: No matter what the Bible says, waiting is hard. Though God says that it's good for me to wait quietly on Him, I usually kick and scream instead. After all, why shouldn't I put up a good, honest fight—or at least a vigorous display of self-pity—when I don't get what I want, when I want it? Why wait when I can try to control everything, including God?

My anti-waiting streak isn't merely part of my sinful, rebellious nature. Waiting is downright scary. It has been compared to the temporary panic of the trapeze artist in midair. With reckless trust, one trapeze artist must fling herself from the security of her rung to the uncertainty of being caught by her partner on the other. But in the meantime, for a split second, she is suspended in the air between the two. Will the strong hand of her partner grab and hold on? It's a terrifying moment.

Waiting on God is the in-between time, the time of panic, when our lives seem frozen in midair for a month, a year, a decade. God leads us to let go of the first rung. Often, we resist God's plan, clutching tightly to safety. If we're forced to let go, we push God for instant resolution. So we fight, we sulk, we resist this uncomfortable work of God's grace.

HURTING

Waiting is not only scary; it hurts. I think of my friend, Helen Urback, an eighty-five-year-old woman whose body is wasting away from Parkinson's disease and stomach cancer. She's waiting on God to go home. My friend, Mary, is waiting for spiritual renewal in her church. After years of disunity, gossip, and a lack of outreach, the heart of her church has grown cold and hard. Pockets of revival are beginning to melt the icy center, but at times this progress seems slow and tedious. Or I think of my friend, Tom, who is waiting for God to heal his sexual compulsions. Now he's seeking Christ for purity of heart.

Through tears, Helen, Mary and Tom have each asked me the same question: "Why does it take so long? How long must I wait?" We often sidestep such painful questions, seeking to minimize the hurt and pushing people toward our flawed conception of instant maturity. "Just get over it," we exhort others—or ourselves. From God's perspective, however, my friends' questions are entirely legitimate. "How long, O LORD? Will you forget me forever? How long will you hide your face from me?" the psalmist cried (Psalm 13:1). Even as believers in Christ, Paul says we "groan inwardly as we wait eagerly for our adoption as sons, the redemption of our bodies" (Romans 8:23). God doesn't expect us to minimize the hurt of our waiting. He knows we will groan.

The first stages, fighting and hurting, may not feel like the "correct" or "spiritually mature" way to wait. For most of us, however, fighting and hurting are simply honest responses to this hard gift. Even as we mature, we will still fight and groan when we are forced to wait. It is simply a condition of life here and now. Fortunately, however, these two difficult stages are not the end of the process on our journey toward maturity.

RECEIVING

What can we do besides fight and hurt? As did my friend, Bill, we can learn to receive from God. For many years Bill was a successful, self-employed engineer. Professionally, he never had to wait for anything. He simply made things happen. As a new Christian, he approached his faith with the same kind of let's-make-it-happen-now attitude. Until, that is, his business went bankrupt and he fell into the deep pit of clinical depression. A quick-fix approach to his problems did not work, even with faith in God and a bottle of antidepressants.

As do many of us, Bill assumed that having to wait was a sign of failure. For the first time in his life, he couldn't achieve his way out of a problem. After five months of prayer, Bible reading, counseling, medication, and simply being loved by other believers, Bill is learning to be still and to receive from God.

Psalm 131:2 describes Bill's journey: "I have stilled and quieted my soul; like a weaned child with its mother, like a weaned child is my soul within me." This is a beautiful picture of a man who knows that his life is sheltered in God's love. After struggling and striving, the psalmist, as did my friend, finally learned to rest in God's love, to enjoy intimacy with God. In this sense, waiting becomes an invitation from God to rest, to receive grace.

"When God brings a time of waiting, advised Oswald Chambers, "Don't fill it with busyness, just wait." I took exactly the opposite approach. Waiting caused me to feel awkward, unproductive, and even useless. I don't know how many times I told my wife, "I feel as if I've been put on the shelf." My solution? Get busy. Make things happen. Fill the emptiness with productivity.

Ever so slowly, I'm learning to adjust the rhythms of my soul to God's gift of waiting. What do we do while we "just wait?" First and foremost, we receive. During our waiting times, God seems to whisper, "Be like a weaned child: content, quiet, satisfied. Be still. I have you here for a reason. Don't strive to achieve, just receive." While we wait, we can learn to receive God's presence in our lives in a deeper way than we've experienced before.

CHANGING

C. S. Lewis referred to the process of sanctification as "undragoning." In his novel, *The Voyage of the Dawn Treader,* we meet a very unsanctified boy named Eustace. By sleeping on the dragon's hoard "with greedy, dragonish thoughts in his heart," Eustace became a lonely and miserable dragon.

Aslan the lion, who represents Christ in this story, instructs Eustace to take off his outer scales. Though he does his best to shed his scaly "clothes," as soon as Eustace removes one layer of his dragon self, another appears. Near despair, he asks, "How ever many skins have I got to take off?" It is then that Aslan says gently, "You will have to let me undress you."

The first tear from Aslan's claws "hurt worse than anything I've ever felt," Eustace would later tell his friends. Then, even though he was tender and sore, Aslan threw him into a pool of water. At first, "it smarted like anything," but in a short time, Eustace realized that he had become a real boy again.

The New Testament writers knew the connection between waiting and the "undragoning" process. "Perseverance [waiting on God] must finish its work so that you may be mature and complete, not lacking anything" (James 1:4). If we accept waiting as a gift, God will use it to transform our souls, undragoning our old selves and clothing us with the character of Christ.

The journal entries, during my two-year wait, record many moments when I struggled to recognize waiting as God's work in my life. In September 1994, I wrote:

God, I feel lost, confused, and stuck...And yet, I know You are using this time to burn away the dross of selfishness, impatience, and immaturity. It is incredible that I have been so numb to my own sin.

Six months later I wrote:

God, I hate waiting for Your direction, but I know You are softening my hard heart.

Unfortunately, from our perspective, our waiting can seem useless and unproductive. Nothing appears to be happening. Spiritual growth seems to stand still. From God's perspective, however, waiting deepens and widens our souls. It is often through these apparently arid seasons that God changes us, digging up hidden sins, cultivating spiritual fruit, shaping our character, and lavishing us with grace. As we wait, there will be moments when we catch glimpses of the changes God is working in our hearts. Sometimes, however, the full scope of the changes God has wrought in us will not be apparent until much later.

WATCHING

"So is waiting a completely passive process?" we may ask in protest. "Isn't there something I can do while I wait?"

Yes, there is an active role for us: We can become watchmen. "I wait for the LORD, my soul waits," declared the psalmist. "My soul waits for the LORD more than watchmen wait for the morning" (Psalm 130:5-6).

What is a watchman? In biblical times, watchmen vigilantly guarded the city. They watched for enemies who might attack at night, and they waited for the sun to come up. They were alert and obedient, ready to respond when needed. When called upon, they sprang into action. But on the other hand, watchmen didn't make things happen. They didn't control the rising of the sun. They couldn't speed up the process. A watchman knew the difference between his job and God's job.

Using the watchman as a benchmark, Eugene Peterson contends,

> *Waiting does not mean doing nothing. It is not fatalistic resignation. It means going about our assigned tasks, confident that God will provide the meaning and the conclusions. . . . It means a confident and alert expectation that God will do what He said He will do.*

During our two-year holding pattern, waiting placed a tremendous strain on our marriage. I became impatient and angry, directing much of my frustration at my wife. She, in turn, slid into a deep depression. Each of us began to withdraw emotionally from the other. Our hearts were wounded, and our marriage was in jeopardy.

What could I do? Like most men, I tried to fix things. First, I tried to fix my career confusion. Another goal came in a close second: fix my marriage. Heroically, I took things into my own hands. Unfortunately, the more I tried to fix and control every-thing—including my wife—the more chaotic things became, pushing my wife into emotional orbit.

Somewhere in the midst of my impatient, hardheaded efforts, God helped me begin to understand what it means to be a watch-man, to wait patiently for Him. Fixing and controlling the situa-tion were like trying to expedite the rising of the sun. I reflected on Eugene Peterson's description of the watchman's attitude—"a confident and alert expectation that God will do what He said He will do"—and began to release things into God's hands. I active-ly entrusted my career, my wife's emotions, my impatience, and my wounded marriage to His timing. "Stop controlling and fix-ing everything," the Spirit seemed to say. "That's not your job. I will lead you and heal you—in My timing, not yours. For your part, wait and watch."

The healing didn't come overnight. But as I began to assume the role of a watchman, both my wife and I have experienced what Isaiah promised for those who wait on God: "No ear has perceived, no eye has seen any God besides you, who acts on behalf of those who wait for him" (Isaiah 64:4). Three years ago, I never could have imagined the healing work of Christ in our marriage and in our souls. Such is the power of being a watch-man—praying, remaining alert, obeying God where we can, and trusting Him to "provide the meaning and the conclusions."

ON EAGLES' WINGS

Sometimes I still struggle to remember that it's good to wait qui-etly for the Lord. It isn't easy. It goes against the grain of my fall-en soul and my quick-fix culture. At times it still hurts to wait. But there's also a gift from God hidden in the waiting. I have an opportunity to receive from God, to allow Christ to change my soul, to watch for the wonders of God's work in my life.

Now I can see the seasons of waiting that once sapped my spirit of vitality can also be God's gift to revitalize my soul. "Those who wait for the LORD," Isaiah promised, "shall renew their strength, they shall mount up with wings like eagles, they shall run and not be weary, they shall walk and not faint" (Isaiah 40:31).

CHAPTER 3

"Whenever you pray, go into your room and

shut the door and pray to your Father who is

in secret; and your Father who sees in secret

will reward you.

"When you are praying, do not heap up

empty phrases....for your Father knows what

you need before you ask him."

MATTHEW 6:6-8 *(NRSV)*

Praying by Heart

Your disciples requested, "Lord, teach us to pray,"
and You responded with a model for all ages—
simple and straightforward.
How could we hope to sway with form and fluency
the one Who orders galaxies and oceans?
And so we pray as You taught them—and us.
First, we proclaim the parenthood of God...
accept both rank and duty inherent in that claim,
and then, petitioning, we pray for basic things:
bread for the body, bread for the spirit,
acceptance of the two-edged blessing of forgiveness;
admission of our weakness, our dependency,
our chronic need for guidance.
And then we close as we began, in praise.
How fitting, Lord, that You Who feed Your sheep
and tend Your vineyard—simple employments—
disdain the ostentation of those who pray toward earthly,
rather than heavenly ears.
May all our prayers be simple and direct...
wrenched from our heart,
and bleeding with our need.

EVELYN MINSHULL

Newfound Power in the Prayer That Jesus Taught Us

One night, several years ago, a telephone call woke me out of a deep sleep. That was the night I began an adventure, a spiritual adventure, that goes on to this day. It involves a new, highly personal approach to the most beautiful, most familiar, most powerful prayer of all—The Lord's Prayer.

The call came about midnight. "I'm calling for Mona," said an unfamiliar voice. "Mona wanted me to tell you that Walt has had a massive heart attack. They're in an ambulance on their way to San Luis. Mona says, 'Pray for us.'"

Has it ever happened to you that, with a sudden shock, the well of prayer within you seems dry? It happened to me that night. I simply couldn't find words. All I could do was think of beautiful Mona, my closest spiritual friend, sitting beside the stricken form of her artist husband. I pictured the ambulance, racing from their studio in the California coast village of Cambria, to the city of San Luis Obispo thirty-five miles south.

"Pray for us," was Mona's message to me—but no prayer came.

"Help me to pray," I murmured to God. Quick as lightning some words flashed in my mind: *Pray The Lord's Prayer.* And like the echoing thunder my mind rejected them. "No use," I chided my subconscious. "I say The Lord's Prayer every day. It doesn't speak to the condition." Again the words came, more insistent, with additional emphasis: *PRAY The Lord's Prayer.*

Ah! That caught my attention. Say The Lord's Prayer. Pray The Lord's Prayer. Starting then I began to discover that there was a very real difference. That night I prayed His Prayer rather than simply repeating it like a child reciting the ABCs.

While I was praying, Mona and Walt were arriving at the hospital in San Luis. The prognosis for Walt was dire. Physicians, looking at a man past sixty who'd not only suffered a heart attack but had three clots in his lungs, pneumonia and a temperature of 107 degrees, believed he would not last the night.

But he did. And he lived for two years after that, fully active, then passed on quietly in his sleep. Those two years were a physical victory for Walt, but the telling point was spiritual. Walt had been a borderline agnostic. After that night, he and Mona at last shared spiritual treasure, for, she told me, "there was a complete change in his attitude toward God."

Was this coincidence or could it have been related to the power of The Lord's Prayer as I had prayed it? I had to believe the latter because, as I continued to pray it daily, the fruitage in my personal life was rich, satisfying, often unexpected. For example: An ugly tumor, scheduled for surgery, simply disappeared from my finder; it had been growing there since I slammed the finger in a car door. A financial crisis and a family squabble of some duration both evaporated without my taking thought. One afternoon when I picked up my granddaughter at school in answer to a "sick call," she was feverish, manifesting all the flu symptoms. While we drove I prayed as I was learning to do—and saw a normal child replace a sick one before my very eyes.

So how do you learn to pray The Lord's Prayer? Here are a few suggestions I offer from my own experience:

One: I found that it takes less than sixty seconds (even in church) to say the prayer, and anywhere from ten minutes to half an hour to pray it.

Two: There is no way to pray this prayer for one person or one family alone. The minute I consciously addressed "Our Father," even though my immediate concern was Walt and Mona, I was also including my family, friends, strangers, enemies—those who had "passed on" and those yet to arrive. I was praying for them as well. As I contemplated this I realized the universal intent of Christ when He gave the prayer to us.

Three: I had to be willing to be taught how to pray this prayer on a daily basis. I accepted the Holy Spirit as my guide and tried faithfully to follow the readings that came to me. Some days I was moved to use a Bible concordance to gain understanding. In phrases like *Thy kingdom come, Thy will be done*, I looked up keywords—*kingdom, will*—and meditated on what Jesus taught about them. Or I turned to the dictionary and looked up *forgive, debts, trespasses*. Sometimes I found myself simply praying it as a psalm of praise and adoration. But day by day, it yielded new insights.

Four: I came to recognize it as a complete prayer, nothing left out. In my newspaper days, I was taught that a complete story answers the questions who, where, when, why, what. As I meditated on The Lord's Prayer, I found that it spoke to all conditions.

When we pray, "Thy kingdom come, Thy will be done on earth as it is in heaven," we make supplication not only for our own known and unknown needs but also for the needs of His children everywhere. This, to me, was the source of those unexpected results in my own experience—the healing of my finger, my finances, my family relationships—without taking thought. The implications on a worldwide scale were overwhelming.

Five: There was something I had to do to become a clear channel for this power. *Forgive us as we forgive...* Forgive meant to "give up resentment against or the desire to punish; to stop being angry with." Debtors were those who I felt "owed" me something, including certain behavior, such as respect, affection, gratitude. Trespassers had "wronged" me in some way, violated my territory, encroached, invaded. To my surprise, I found those I felt had "wronged" me fewer than those who *owed* me, but it made me aware of what I considered trespasses. I came to believe that every time I made a judgment about someone, or criticized or just plain gossiped. I was trespassing.

So I made lists and worked diligently on full aspects of forgiveness. It hasn't been quick or easy. In fact, I find I have to keep working at it. But with the doing has come great freedom—and peace, and the release of healing into all my relationships.

Six: I found I had to come to terms with the unexpected. Although I was learning alone, I often felt I was praying with the Master and His disciples in Galilee, and they were praying with me. Or I seemed to enter into the body of prayer, beyond or above time, so to speak, of which everyone who had ever prayed these words was still a part—and the sense of unity and power in that body of prayer was awesome.

Seven: As the prayer became part of my day's consciousness, there was a bonus of grace that continued after I had finished the actual praying; an aura of pleasure and peace clung to me hour by hour. It changed my days as dramatically as though a black-and-white world had been transformed into living color. If I was tempted to let it fade, something would surface to recall me.

One day, when I was caught in a crush at a department store sale, an unlikely recollection popped into my head: Chief Justice Oliver Wendell Holmes had once said that his whole religion could be summed up in the first two words of The Lord's Prayer. Fleetingly, as I dodged a flying elbow, I wondered, *Why that thought now?* Of course! *Our Father.* As I repeated it there, I saw that these unruly people were His children, just as I was, and my panic subsided. I made my way calm and unscathed to an exit. Or, when faced with a personal crisis, I would find that magnificent affirmation. *Thine is the kingdom and the power and the glory* rising to reassure me.

Less dramatically I found myself given a single word to say over and over that seemed to keep the contact open. It is a very old word, one used by Moses, by Jesus, by Paul, by all Christians today. But it had been renewed for me by my studies. It means "hearty agreement, steadfastness, truthfulness." It means "So be it!... So it is." It is praise, thanksgiving, blessing. Our Lord used it to close His Prayer. I would like to use it now as a benediction for all of us who attempt to pray His Prayer. Amen.

When Memory Serves

Darlene Seegert

I scanned the dining hall, trying to spot Mom in the sea of gray. Elderly men and women, their faces deeply lined, sat clustered at tables of four.

Mom was near a corner, her wispy white hair set off by her blue sweater. I walked over and gave her a hug and a big smile. She didn't say hello, but from the way she pursed her lips, I knew she recognized me.

Since her stroke six months earlier, Mom needed help remembering things—her grandchildren's names, what year it was, names of colors, how to count to twenty. Later that night as I helped her get ready for bed, she seemed to be back in her childhood.

"Is the milking done yet?" she asked. "Are the cows in from the barn?"

"Mom, you're in a nursing home now. You're not on the farm."

She stared at me blankly, trying to understand. She started to cry. Nothing I said or did consoled her. I gave up trying to settle her down and took to pushing her in her wheelchair back and forth in the hallway.

That's when I spotted the boy and his grandfather. Three rooms away from Mom's, a boy about eight years old knelt by his grandpa's bed. They were praying out loud.

Why hadn't I thought of that? In earlier years Mom recited the Lord's Prayer countless times, at everything from children's baptisms to confirmations. At my father's funeral, I remembered Mom dabbing tears from her eyes with a lace handkerchief as the minister prayed it.

Back in her room, I asked, "Would you like to pray?"

Her tired eyes met mine. "Oh, yes," she said. She sat up straight in her wheelchair, folded her hands and bowed her head.

"Our Father," I began. "Who art in heaven," she joined in, never stumbling or pausing. The knot in her brow softened and her face relaxed. Once more I glimpsed the mom who had bandaged my knees, wiped my eyes and told me everything would be all right.

From that night on, Mom and I prayed together each time before I went home. Not once did she lose interest. Not once was she too confused to continue. When I left in the evenings and said, "I'll see you tomorrow," she lay her head on the pillow and put her trust in the Lord.

Sudden Fury

Kim Engelmann

My husband, Tim, and I like to take our pocket Bible with us when we go camping. In the evening we read aloud to each other from Psalms. Over the years I've come to memorize many verses, repeating them over and over in my mind. But I would never have guessed the strange power of one verse that came to me on a camping trip in New York's Adirondacks.

We had arrived at the ranger station around noon. It was a beautiful, clear fall day. The leaves were just turning, and the vistas were spectacular. We parked our car and registered with the ranger. He described the area to us, telling us about local landmarks and sights we'd see on our hike in the wilderness to the campground. He gave us a brief warning about bears.

"If you see a bear at your campground, just clang some metal pots together, give a yell and the bear will run away." He advised.

Neither Tim nor I was particularly alarmed. We put on our backpacks and began the six-mile hike up to the campground. No other campers were on the trail. It was so quiet we could hear the leaves crunching beneath our feet.

Tim and I relished the solitude. Back in the New York City area, we were both full-time graduate students, commuting to different schools. Now we were grateful to have a few days together away from classes, textbooks and term papers.

We reached camp, just below the timberline, at sunset and set up our tent in the waning light. The moon came out and the air was cool and still. By a roaring fire we ate our dinner and spent a while reading from Psalms in our pocket Bible. Then we put the rest of our food away in our backpacks and hung them from the half-dead branch of a tall, spindly tree, out of the reach of scavenging rodents. The last thing I did was mix some instant chocolate pudding and bring it into our tent before going to bed. Tim and I were soon fast asleep in our sleeping bags, worn out from the hike.

Suddenly something woke me. "What's that noise?" I asked Tim. "A raccoon?" I glanced at the luminescent dial of our alarm clock. It was 2:00 A.M.

Tim sat up and grabbed the flashlight he had left by the tent door. "Too big for a raccoon," he mumbled, half-asleep. "Look," he whispered.

The moon was bright, the sky clear, and with the flashlight I could make out a furry creature shuffling about the campsite. I grinned. "A baby bear," I said. "He's adorable."

We watched as he tried to overturn the stones that had formed the semicircle around our campfire. Disappointed at not finding any food, he lumbered over to the base of the tree that held our backpacks. For a moment the cub disappeared behind a thicket, and we could hear only a few grunts and the tree groaning.

Then came a sudden snap, and our backpacks fell from the broken branch to the ground with a loud thud. Frightened, the cub fled the scene, cracking twigs and kicking up leaves as he left. Then all was quiet. Late-summer crickets chirped.

"I'd better try to hang up those backpacks," Tim said. "The food in them will be a real invitation to raccoons if I leave them there."

"Okay." I slipped back into the warmth of the sleeping bag.

"I wish I had some rope to tie them up with." Tim said.

"We might have some—" I began drowsily. I never finished my sentence. We felt the vibrations of heavy running footsteps, then deep growling. Tim froze. I grabbed his arm.

"The mother bear," he said in a hushed tone as he peered outside. "She's in the camp. She's enormous and she's mad. I think we scared her baby."

We sat petrified and listened as the huge bear began tearing apart our campsite. Pots and pans came clattering down on the rocks. The growling grew more intense. Then she found our backpacks lying on the ground. We heard the dull rip of the canvas bags and the long, searing scream of the zipper as she tore open the metal teeth with her claws.

"Quick, grab some pots and pans and yell!" I said, remembering the ranger's advice. Tim picked up a saucepan and the metal bowl with some of my leftover pudding in it. I could smell the sweet aroma of hardened chocolate in the pan, and it flashed through my mind how bears are drawn to sweets.

Clang, clang, went the makeshift cymbals. "Get outta here," Tim bellowed. "Go on, now! Get!"

The bear responded, but not the way we expected. She started growling, then blasted forth with a violent roar. I scrambled out of the sleeping bag and crouched next to Tim, who fumbled for a small Swiss Army knife and clenched it in his hand. The ground trembled beneath us, and I realized in a split second that she was coming toward us.

Another deafening roar and she was outside the tent, so close that I could smell her breath. It was like rotting garbage. The wall of the tent bulged as the bear pushed against it.

And then as Tim and I clung to each other in terror, I found myself saying some words out loud. "No evil shall befall you." I didn't know why I said them, but even then I knew they came from Psalms. "No evil shall befall you," I kept repeating as the bear began circling the tent. "No evil shall befall you." It was as though I were drawing a protective circle around us.

Then an amazing thing happened. A breeze began to blow. It rustled the few leaves hanging on the tips of the trees. Bushes whispered and the forest wood creaked. The mother bear, who had been roaring furiously, paused for a moment. Upwind of our tent and scent, she stopped in her tracks. For a few moments she was silent. Then she barged off into the brush.

The next morning we surveyed the damage the bear had done. The camp was in shambles, debris strewn everywhere. Our food was gone. The bear had actually chewed up and swallowed most of the glass jar in which we had stored our honey. Only one corner of the jar remained.

On the ground I found our pocket Bible with a bite taken out of it and three long claw marks scratched into the leather cover. I picked it up and thumbed through it, looking for the Bible passage that had come to me so mysteriously the night before. There it was in Psalm 91. But what particularly amazed me was the second half of the verse, appropriate beyond reason for the two of us huddled in our tent. "No evil shall befall you, no scourge come near your tent" (Psalm 91:10, *RSV*).

These days Tim and I still go on camping trips. As usual, we take our Bible along and we always read Psalms by the campfire. And if I ever doubt the power of Scripture, I only have to look at the outside of our "Bear Claw Bible." Three long claw marks and one bite in the corner are evidence enough.

Don't Tell Grandma

Cecile Bauer

Mother and I were sitting at her kitchen table, talking about the family, when suddenly she fixed me with her stern glare. "Something's bothering you, Daughter," she said. "What is it?"

"Wh—what do you mean?" I stammered.

"I know something's wrong."

She was right. Something *was* wrong. Our son was having marital problems, but I didn't want to worry her. Now that she was in her eighties, our family wanted to protect her from the scuffs and scrapes of everyday life. My two older sisters, our husbands and children, even our own grandchildren, had agreed to keep family problems away from her.

Unmarried daughter expecting a baby? Don't tell Grandma. Son stationed in war-torn Middle East? Don't tell Grandma. Grandchildren having problems in school? Don't worry Grandma.

In her own life—encompassing two world wars and one Depression—she'd had problems enough.

When Grandma was a girl, her young mother had died and left her in charge of two brothers and three sisters. One disabled brother died the following year. Later her father was killed by the family bull.

"I don't tell you when there's something wrong because I don't want to worry you," I explained.

"Worry? Right now," she said, "It's all this uncertainty that worries me. I think that someone dear to us has died. I count my grandchildren and great-grandchildren. Did someone have an accident? Does someone have cancer? Nothing could be as bad as what I'm imaging right now."

So I told her about my daughter-in-law leaving my son and the children. "I never intended to hurt you, Mother. I wanted to keep you happy."

"Happiness," she said, "comes from being needed. I can help you with your problems. If you need money, I can lend it. If you need advice, I can give it. And if money or advice won't help, I can pray for you. An old woman alone has plenty of extra time for prayers."

I looked around at the neat kitchen, at the polished wood-grained table that could always expand to hold more people. How many had it held in her younger days, ten, twelve, fifteen? There was always room for one more hungry soul at Mother's table.

"I go to church several times a week. You'd be surprised at what I pray for, Daughter. I pray that Betty will sell her house so she can retire. I pray that you will have success in your writing career. Now I will pray that your son and his wife will settle their differences."

And so Mother again became a member of her own family, a family who needed her and her prayers.

A Little Like Lazarus

Wendy Wilson Greer

A little over ten years ago I was dragged into a far country by a devastating and crippling depression. It lasted for two very, very long years. It was an unbelievable time of anguish and lostness. I was unable to concentrate on anything, to communicate on any level, to laugh or to cry, to appreciate beauty in nature, music, art or literature, to listen to music or to play the piano, to sleep more than an hour or two a night, and worst of all, I was unable to give or to receive love. I felt totally alienated from everyone, especially God. My life had no meaning, no focus, no purpose.

This was a shattering experience for someone who had always excelled! In high school, I won far too many honors. In my university class of 1650 graduates, two awards were given to women. I won them both. I went on to win a prestigious teaching fellowship at a top music school; my faculty advisor said I was one of the best students he had ever had.

A few years later I married a wonderful man who has blessed me incredibly for thirty-five years. We have three marvelous, bright, creative children who have brought us enormous joy. For many years I taught music, chaired benefits, served on various boards, organized and taught church school classes, and took on

110

more and more responsibilities. In short, I thought I was very successful, very productive, but far too busy.

However, during my two-year depression, I was unable to do anything but the basic household tasks and these very badly. I spent ninety percent of my time lying on my bed or on the sofa, immobilized, staring blankly at the ceiling. I looked really scary. My eyes were sunk deep into my sockets from lack of sleep. I have never been thin in my life, but I lost thirty-five pounds without even trying. Most of my friends dropped me; they didn't know what to do. And I felt God had totally abandoned me.

Although I had faithfully attended church all my life, I no longer wanted to go to church. I was unable to pray or to read my Bible. But how fortunate I was, for God blessed me with a faithful, prayerful, loving husband, who *made* me say The Lord's Prayer and the 23rd Psalm every night, after which he would pray the benediction and his own beautiful heartfelt prayers. He insisted that I go to church with him each Sunday. He never gave up on me.

During this time I was hospitalized three times for six or seven weeks each time. I tried to take my life because I felt I was such a burden to my family. I felt I was in quicksand and that I was dragging my family members down with me. I thought they would be so much better off without me. My suicide would be a sacrifice for them. I also had frequent panic attacks over money because of all my medical bills. I feared there wouldn't be enough money left for our youngest child to go to college. Needless to say, I felt like a total failure.

Although I felt completely alienated form God, I didn't realize that all this time God was searching for me. God was closer than ever, trying to bring me home to the place where I could hear the voice calling me the Beloved.

After two horrific years, God found me in the most unlikely

place imaginable—in a first class Hilton hotel in Brussels, of all places! I was feeling a little better by this time, but I was still crippled by depression. My husband had been asked by his law firm to visit their Brussels office. We flew to Brussels, and during the day, I was taken around to see various sights, while he met with the staff in the office. Each evening we were entertained graciously, and by the time we went to bed, we were totally exhausted. One night, in the middle of the night, I awoke from a deep, deep sleep, and I saw a figure of light, a figure of white, gliding from the window to the end of my bed. The figure paused there, and I *knew* that I had been healed. *I knew* that I had been forgiven. *I knew* that I was loved. I felt the peace which passes all understanding, and for the first time in my life, I understood the true meaning of grace.

Although I was awake for the rest of the night, I was unable to tell my husband what had happened when he woke up. I was completely mystified! I kept thinking, why me? I have failed so badly in so many ways. What worse thing could I have done than attempt to take my life? Why would God choose to heal me when I felt so out of touch spiritually?

Finally, on the second morning when we were eating breakfast in our room overlooking Brussels, my husband started to turn the BBC News on. I said, "Wait, turn it off! I have to talk with you." He looked at me and said, "What's with you? I have never seen you look so happy." I told him about the holy figure, tears streaming down my face. My husband, who had been the one who had prayed so beautifully for my healing night after night for two years, looked at me and said, "Oh, it was probably the maid in her white uniform coming in to do something she had neglected to do earlier!"

I couldn't believe what I was hearing and said, "At 2:00 A.M.?" Since the astonishing experience, my life has never been the same. It has been totally transformed, turned upside down. All the things I thought were important no longer seemed important—what I did, how successful I was, what people said about me, how I looked, or how much money I had—all the outward, worldly signs. When those were stripped away, the one thing that was left was my little, tiny soul—my little, tiny battered soul. But it was alive, and it was kept alive by the faithfulness of my beloved husband and other prayerful people. It was my soul that mattered most; it was my soul that was priceless.

After we returned to New York, I would rise early each morning to pray and read my Bible, tears often streaming down my face. My teenage son would come in for breakfast and put his hand on my shoulder and say lovingly, "What is it today?" I would reply, "It just seems that God wrote these words specifically for me, that God is speaking directly to me." Each passage gave me unbelievable inspiration and comfort. Each day was a gift I never expected to have. Each friend was more precious because I didn't think I had many friends.

One night a year later, when my husband and I were having a candlelit dinner alone, I looked at him and said, "Why are you smiling like that?" "Oh," he replied, "It is just wonderful to see you so happy!" And I said, "I must have been really hard to live with during the past year." I was overflowing with gratitude, love, hope, confidence and joy. He answered lovingly, "Yes, it was a little bit like living with Lazarus!" But you see, in a real sense, I had been dead, and I was alive again. I had been lost—so lost— but had been found. I was constantly rejoicing, and I know God was too.

The Heart of Prayer

Van Varner

It was a day of anguish. For months my mother had been ill; for weeks she had been suffering agony from the cancer that was killing her, and today was the day when she was returning to the hospital. I was preparing to leave the office to take her there when my executive editor called me for a conference.

"I'd like you to do an article on the subject of 'When to Pray,'" he said to me. "Why don't you consider Paul's exhortation to Pray without ceasing? (Thessalonians 5.17) You might even try it for a day and see what it means to you."

It was difficult to think of exploring an article while deeply concerned with something else, but this assignment was obviously fitting to the circumstances. If anything, it was too fitting; the events of this day could not be interpreted as proper examples of routine living. Still, the idea was challenging.

As I arranged last-minute details in my office, a fellow editor dropped in, and very casually and skillfully (I realized later) told me something quite funny. I laughed. And when it came to me that I was laughing, I said my first prayer—a prayer of gratitude for good humor, which can keep us all in balance, and for this friend who had come purposely to cheer.

Down on the street, I saw a father bawling out his son, who, in turn, was responding with squealing argument. I said a prayer for them that each should find understanding and respect. A newspaper headline yelled out at me about a teenage killer. I prayed for him, and for the two families. My taxicab driver complained about the summer heat. I prayed for him too.

In my mother's apartment the nurse moved about silently, now laying out a dress, now gathering together the few essentials for the hospital suitcase. Briefly, as I watched her, my appreciation for her care and vigilance was translated into prayer, and then my thoughts returned to Mother. It was not easy to present myself as calm and assured, to act as though this journey to the hospital was a good thing, that there the terrible pain would be softened. In my own mind I was not sure.

It had been two weeks since the specialist in charge of her case had gone on vacation; his substitute had not telephoned or visited since then. A faithful general practitioner had come daily, but still I worried for fear Mother was not receiving sufficient attention. She was unable to take any sedative stronger than aspirin, and her pain was constant and excruciating. Finally I had taken it upon myself to call the substituting specialist and suggest hospitalization. The doctor felt the idea had merit and said he would telephone the general practitioner about it, and would come to see Mother. A day later he had done neither, and so I made arrangements without him.

Father, guide me. Help me to have acted wisely.

Father, give my mother strength for this short but difficult trip.

She had the strength and, in fact, seemed to benefit from the sun and air and change of locale. While the hospital made its inaugural tests and Mother was wheeled away for x-rays, I went downstairs to brood over a cup of coffee. There I found myself in conversation with a woman who was obviously under great strain.

"My son," she said to me, "Was operated on two days ago. He's fine, they say, but I worry so much and I stay here all day. He's only twenty-one, too young to have a hernia."

I thought of my mother, who seemed young to me, at sixty—at any age—to be riddled with cancer, and I became annoyed by this woman's monologue. Then I remembered my pledge to pray unceasingly, and I addressed God again, this time for a young man's return to robust activity, and for the easing of his mother's deep distress.

By the time I had left the coffee shop, I actually recognized a kind of tranquility within myself, and thereby made a vital discovery about prayer. My sudden peace of mind was, I believe, directly related to being absorbed in the problems of another. "Dwell on your own peril and you may be reduced to gibbering panic," Fulton Oursler once wrote in an article about finding presence of mind. "Think of others and you may well find yourself doing the precisely correct thing." This is what prayer offers as well.

For the remainder of the afternoon Mother and I talked cheerfully together, and then, as the emergency painkiller she had taken at home lost its potency, the agony returned, vengefully. It was hours before she was quiet again. By then I had been called into the hall by a new surgeon. The x-rays had revealed a desperate condition. The doctors told me that my mother could not live more than twenty-four hours without an operation, and there was little chance of her surviving that.

I do not know whether they were asking permission to operate or not. I simply looked at them. What other course of action could there be?

In the warmth and murkiness of the night, I sat beside my mother and held her left hand as she drowsed. Her other hand was strapped to a board while liquid strength flowed into her veins. *I must pray,* I told myself.

But I could not. Pray without ceasing? I couldn't pray at all. It was simple to pray for cab drivers and ladies with vigorous sons, but pray for my mother's life? I could not ask that much of Him.

The minutes melded into a quarter-hour, then a half, and my mind seemed empty. Slowly, without rationalizing, without focusing my thoughts at all, I began to repeat the same inaudible words to her: *Love and contentment...love and contentment....*

I don't know where the words came from, but they were there to the exclusion of everything else. It was as though I wanted to swath my mother in love, to bring her utter comfort, and that by keeping her hand in mine I could transfuse the power of those silent words.

The night passed and early the next morning surgery was performed. Mother underwent it successfully, as I knew somehow she would.

That afternoon as I returned home to sleep, my prayers diminished in gratitude as a feeling of anger took their place—anger against the doctor who might have come and who might have foreseen the critical situation. I was in a white fury when I telephoned him. I castigated him for what I considered was his dereliction of duty, and when he replied with what I thought were lame excuses, I swore at him. What had happened to my praying without ceasing? The past twenty-four hours had been challenging ones and I had failed to pass muster. I could pray in situations that did not touch me near, but I was not prepared for those that struck the raw nerve of emotion. In retrospect, I recognized the value and importance of formal periods of prayer, be they in church, upon rising or going to bed, in specific quiet moments. I believe now, however, that just as a man should not be a Sunday Christian only, neither should he restrict himself only to a prayer schedule. When Paul said *pray without ceasing* he was, of course, saying that God should be foremost in man's mind at all times, but more, he was offering man a practical instrument—prayer—for accomplishing this end. He was prescribing a conduct of life that would include all eventualities.

The athlete who does not train cannot expect victory. Similarly, a man who does not practice praying may expect to find his control weakened when he needs to call upon it.

"It is," Alex Carrel said, "when prayer becomes a habit that it operates on the character." Prayer and God are not sometime things.

"Love and contentment" was a prayer from deep within me. It came unconsciously when I thought myself empty. The oaths I flung at the doctor, however, represented a collapse of the prayer fabric because I did not care. Had I been prepared by a life of praying, had I learned the value of silence in which prayer is most effective, I believe I would not have sworn at that physician. I most certainly would have taken him to task as I saw the facts, but if I had had the resources from which to form prayers, both for him and for my own equanimity, I would not have allowed my argument with him to be dissipated in frenzy.

On a Sunday morning, after two weeks of numb struggle, Mother died. By then, for me, as I am sure it was already for her, the continuity of life had been affirmed. And one of the insights into living that her death had given me was that we come closest to God, who is with us always, in times of prayer. When we pray without ceasing, difficult as it is to achieve, we are with *Him* always.

Gratitude:
The Heart of Grace

Elizabeth Ann Bartlett

A few years ago, I needed a new heart—literally. Little did I know how much receiving a new physical heart would also transform my spiritual heart. The spiritual gifts in the new life I received through my heart transplant have been many—gifts of joy, wonder, compassion, and perhaps more than all the others, gratitude.

Gratitude did not come easily in the years of illness and disability preceding my heart transplant. Stricken with heart failure at a young age (I was thirty-eight), I was angry and overwhelmed by a sense of deprivation of all that had been taken from me—my health, my work, traveling, walking in the woods, gardening, and most devastating, time with my husband and one-year-old son. I was filled with resentment, and that resentment was threatening to poison me. For my own physical, emotional, and spiritual survival, I had to come to see the blessings in this illness. And blessings were there to be found—a slower and saner pace of life, a time for reflection, a learned empathy for the old, the young, the infirm, and the oppressed. This was my first lesson in the transformative power of gratitude, for I found that when I looked for the blessings in this experience of illness, resentment melted away.

The transformative power of gratitude is the power to make of a curse, a blessing; to make an absence, an abundance. I learned this when I focused on what I didn't have. I had a closet full of clothes and nothing to wear, a houseful of books and nothing to read, a life full of opportunity and nothing to do. When I focused on what I did have, the handful of fish and the few loaves of bread became enough to feed a multitude. Thankfulness—an appreciation of what we have fills our lives. When we are grateful we are full—full of gratitude. The gratitude I'm talking about is that of the father for the prodigal son; the gratitude for that which was lost, that now is found; that amazing grace that fills us when something that we feared lost is returned to us. In our losing it, or nearly losing, it becomes all the more precious.

Living as I did with "sudden death syndrome," the possibility of losing my life was a daily presence. As the reality of the tenuousness of my life sank in, I came to see each day as a gift. I lived on the edge of lost and found; every day held the potential of my losing my life, and every day I found life again. This seemed particularly poignant to me each night as I tucked my little boy in his bed, wondering if I would live through the night. As I left his room, I would say, "See you in the morning," more in prayer than in certainty. And I began each day with a "thank you" for living through the night and finding my sweet baby in my arms once more.

This sense of the fragility and preciousness of our time together pervaded our whole family. Thankfulness became a part of our family's daily ritual. Gathering around the table at dinner time, we would hold hands with one another and say grace and that grace always included a thank-you for one more day of being together.

Grace. *Graci. Gracias.* Thank you. We say grace by giving thanks, and what is more, in giving thanks, we find grace. The interweaving of grace and gratitude are so apparent to me now. According to the *Oxford English Dictionary,* grace includes the divine influence to regenerate and sanctify and to impart strength to endure trial and resist temptation. I had been seeking a way to regenerate my spirit, to endure the trials of deprivation and resist the temptations of bitterness and resentment. I had turned to gratitude, and I had found grace. To live in grace is to be living in a state of gratitude, gratitude for the ordinary things of life—the colors of the sunrise, clean water to drink, a warm hug, the first stars of evening. A daily appreciation of the ever-present gifts of our lives, so easily taken for granted, grants us grace. Living in the fullness of such gratitude, we have little room for greed, resentment, or hostility. I know that even at my grumpiest, a remembrance of the gifts of my life will quickly restore in me the fullness and joy of gratitude. Of grace.

Sometimes I think the real gift I received in receiving the new heart is the gift of knowing gratitude in such a deep and profound way, for it was with my literal change of heart that I became vividly aware that what once had been lost now was found. Gratitude filled me and flowed from me, gratitude for the daily gifts I never again want to take for granted—to walk in the woods, to dance, to dive into a clear cool lake, to work up a good sweat, to enter into a passionate discussion, to feel a lightness in my being, to tuck my son in bed at night knowing I'll be there when he wakes up in the morning.

I had the opportunity of nearly losing my life, and having it restored in me in deeper ways. Perhaps I had in a strange way stumbled across the meaning of Jesus' teaching that whomever would find life must first lose it. I had lost so much of my life, and now it was returned to me, and it seemed sevenfold. I was given a new heart, and that precious gift has given me a wonderful life and health, but it has also given me a new spirit—a spirit of gratitude—the heart of grace.

CHAPTER 4

"Again, truly I tell you, if two of you

agree on earth about anything you ask,

it will be done for you

by my Father in heaven.

For where two or three are gathered

in my name,

I am there among them."

MATTHEW 18:19-20 *(NRSV)*

Where Two or Three Are Gathered

Lord,

Lay on my heart

whom I should pray for today.

Show me how to encourage them, I pray.

Touch someone's heart

to pray for me, too,

and bless our friendship

with each other and You.

NANCIAN DAVIS HALL

How To: Handle Prayer with Care

Denise George

It used to be that my prayers for others, though heartfelt, were offered to God in a rather casual way. I remember the time when a friend suffered a miscarriage and she asked me to pray for her. It was only late at night that I thought of her request. I said a quick prayer and fell asleep. Not until my young son, Christian, entered the hospital for some serious testing did I begin to find a different, more caring way of praying.

When I called my closest friends and asked them to pray for Christian, I was surprised at their response. They didn't just say yes and let it go at that. They asked questions. "What time are the tests?" "What is the nature of the problem?" "Who is his doctor?" "How long will Christian be in the hospital?" Then without fail, each friend called daily with reassurance and support.

During the long, anxious week of Christian's hospitalization, I felt strengthened by their prayers. If I was discouraged or afraid, I would remember that I was not alone. My anxieties were quieted. When Christian finally returned home with a clean bill of health, I thanked God. I also thanked my friends who had taught me something new and important about prayer. Here is some of the advice I gave to myself.

Be specific: If God knows all our needs, why do we need to ask for them by name?

Not for Him—that seems clear—but for ourselves. Any over-whelming task can seem less daunting when we break it down into its components. My mind is inclined to go blank when I pray in generalities, but when I focus on specifics I feel as though I'm making real contact.

Study: At the end of an educational conference, I met a young father and we spoke briefly of his wife, Scotty, and her long, difficult wait for a heart-and-lung transplant. Immediately I promised to pray for her. Then I followed that up by going to the library and reading all I could about such operations. By the time Scotty was finally summoned to the hospital, I knew what the risks and complications might be. When I prayed for her, my understanding was greater, my compassion deeper.

Act: At the weekly meetings of our church guild, the needs of our denomination's missionaries are called out for prayer. Requests range from new water pumps to airplane tickets—often things that we members can do something about. Once a family of medical missionaries asked if we could send them some used prescription eyeglasses. We scurried around and eventually sent off a box full of them. Other groups did the same—enough to provide seven hundred African schoolchildren with glasses.

It has been said that "to work is to pray." I've often thought that deeds like mailing off a box of eyeglasses serve "to put shoe leather" on prayers.

"The real business of your life as a saved soul is intercessory prayer," Oswald Chambers once wrote. For me, I have found that the more I pray for others, the more I care, and the more I care, the better my prayer.

What Prayer Can Do

Harold Hostetler

When we lived in Hawaii some years ago, my wife and I hosted a prayer group in our home. We were a diverse group of ten to twelve people. I was a newspaper reporter. One woman was a musician; another, a schoolteacher. And Arnold, a Navy commander, was in charge of maintaining and repairing nuclear submarines at the U.S. Naval Shipyard at Pearl Harbor.

Arnold had been skeptical when his wife, Carolyn, began attending our group. He just couldn't believe that God paid any attention to individual prayers. But when Carolyn's severe back pains disappeared one evening after we prayed for her, Arnold decided to come along. And he asked us to pray about something he thought impossible.

"I've got a repair job on a sub out there that just baffles all of us," he said. "No matter what we do, the repairs don't work. Can we ask God about that?" We did.

The following week Arnold told our group he had decided how to proceed with the repairs based not on logic but on intuition—a shot in the dark, he called it. He put his crew to work.

That evening as we sat down to pray, the phone rang. The call was for Arnold. As he hung up, his eyes were full of wonder.

"That was my crew," he said. "They just ran the final check on the repairs. Everything works perfectly!"

Arnold's skepticism vanished that night. He knew as well as the rest of us where his "shot in the dark" had come from.

God, I'm Not Finished with My Son!

John Marmonti

On March 6th my fourteen-year-old son, E.J., came home from school with friends, had a snack and proceeded to go out rollerblading around the neighborhood as usual. I was somewhat concerned about him and thought to keep him home since a radio report predicted strong wind gusts of sixty to seventy miles per hour, but he was an experienced skater with years of hockey practice under his belt.

My wife and I were going out food shopping at 5:00 P.M. when a friend came to the door and told us E.J. was hit by a car. At the scene, we came upon an entire city block closed off with police cars, a fire engine, rescue truck and two local ambulances. I got out and ran toward the scene but was stopped by police. Frantically, I said, pointing toward the accident, "That's my son!" but they would not let me go see him. The accident occurred six blocks from a local hospital but it was decided to take him to Children's Hospital in Boston, fifteen miles away. We drove frantically and I remember praying out loud, "God, please don't take my son away from me." I recited every prayer I knew a thousand times over in my mind.

When we arrived we were ushered into a special waiting room

where a social worker told us E.J. was in a coma, had a serious head injury, and had possibly lost one eye. The social worker didn't know about broken bones. E.J. had been hit by a car, flew in the air some thirty feet across a side street, and landed face first on a concrete curb.

Despite E.J.'s unknown condition, we felt the angels had been watching over him. The accident occurred one block from a fire station and within thirty seconds, a trained rescue team arrived. He had stopped breathing, but after a few minutes he was breathing again, and they kept him breathing until the ambulances arrived.

After a few hours and CT scans, E.J. was found to have ten broken facial bones, two large skull fractures and an eye that they thought was lost. While in the ICU, a priest and a nun came by and gave E.J. the last rites. They were very comforting but prayer never hurt so much as then. The bleeding behind the eye prompted them to do eye surgery that night so his eye wouldn't have to be removed. The next morning, to alleviate pressure, he had brain surgery to remove the blood from the fractures in his head. He had no spinal or neck fractures, but we wouldn't know for a while what the outcome would be.

The doctor who took charge of E.J. kept us calm but realistic. E.J. was in ICU hooked up to a breathing machine and had tubes coming out all over him. The second night things were calmer and it all hit me: this was my baby boy and I may lose him. I couldn't stop the tears. I just stared, held his hand, and sobbed.

The nurse, a portly woman of about sixty years, came over and held me for a minute or so and said, "Just keep talking to God. The doctors know their job and it's in God's hands. Tell God you're not finished with your son."

A few minutes later, from the other side of the room behind the curtain, the same nurse sings "Amazing Grace" start to finish, all alone with another patient. I thought God sent me an angel.

During the brain operation, a nun came up to us and said she knew about E.J. "Could she pray for us?" We sat in a small circle of chairs, three of us each holding hands and she prayed on and on. I'll never forget what she said. She asked God to give the doctors healing power and deliver God's healing power through their hands and bring back E.J. to us happy and healthy. After four days in ICU, E.J. started to choke on the breathing tube and move around. They removed the tube and he started breathing on his own. He was then transferred to a rehab hospital for a few days for evaluation and did therapy five hours a day for four months. During that time, he went back to school for an hour a day and sat with his classmates.

His vision came back to his injured eye and he has no physical defects that you can see other than a few fine scars. He passed all the academic tests and is now a healthy sixteen-year-old. His doctor said in all his years he never saw anyone recover from that type of eye injury and the neurosurgeon said with the impact of the accident he should never have survived.

Like that nurse said, "He is in God's hands now. Pray and tell God you're not done with your son yet."

Thank you God for letting me keep my son. I cherish him every day!

Lisa's Baby

Pamela Kumpe

Quietly the voice on the telephone line spoke: "Pam, I need you to pray about something." I recognized the voice as Rhonda's, my friend who had two-year-old twins and went through various fertility treatments to conceive those precious baby girls.

Immediately I responded, "Sure. What is it?"

"Well, my sister Lisa is scheduled to go to Louisiana on Thursday. She has her first appointment with the fertility doctor. Lisa is concerned about the whole process, the cost and her fear of needles. For the past four years she has taken every medical test the doctors can offer and this is the next step. She is over-whelmed by the idea of going through this phase."

"Okay, I will pray for Lisa."

"But," Rhonda paused, "I just want her to be pregnant, right now."

"I'll be glad to pray," I assured her. "Don't worry. I'll lift her up in prayer."

I prayed often and pleadingly for Lisa during the next couple of days. "Dear Lord. As you look down upon Lisa, You see her heart, You know her desire. You can see her need to nurture and bring up a child. Please Lord, as I come before You, grant this prayer request and allow her the opportunity to bring up a child in a godly home." I called another friend, Laura and told her to pray for this special unspoken request.

Picking up my son from school that afternoon, I steered my vehicle down the country road, a shortcut toward our home. "Brandon, we need to pray for someone. There's a woman who wants to have a child. She's tried for a very long time and she really needs our prayers. Will you pray for her with me?"

My thirteen-year-old son held my free hand, bowed his head and prayed. "Dear God, you know this woman Mom is talking about and you know she wants a baby. Help her to have a child. In Jesus' name. Amen."

Just as Brandon finished his prayer and opened his eyes, we both saw a mother cow standing next to what appeared to be a newborn calf across the road in a green pasture. I pressed on the brakes, slowing the car down. We gazed at this heavenly declaration placed before our very eyes. Grinning, I spoke, "Brandon, maybe that's a sign that our friend is pregnant."

Claiming this victory for Lisa, I realized that the Lord does indeed work in mysterious ways and reveals himself to us through many various displays. Very late that night, as my own family slept, I turned on my computer and logged into an online Christian chat room on the Internet. I shared with those present that I had a very important prayer request for a friend who was trying to conceive. A response came up on the screen from a pastor. He used the illustration of Hannah from I Samuel as a place to go for encouragement. Turning to I Samuel to read Hannah's story, the magnitude of her prayer revealed a desperate woman who sought the Lord: "O Lord Almighty, if you will look down upon my sorrow and answer my prayer and give me a son." My heart leaped with joy when I read the Lord's response to Hannah. "May the God of Israel grant the request you have asked of him." Prayer warriors were out in force and seeking God for a miracle.

The next day, Wednesday, Lisa promptly arrived at Rhonda's house for lunch as she often did during the week. In her hand she held a package. She headed to the bathroom and Rhonda immediately knew that Lisa was taking another pregnancy test!

"I just had to take one more test before going to the fertility clinic tomorrow," Lisa announced and disappeared into the bathroom.

As Lisa was taking the pregnancy test in the bathroom at Rhonda's house, prayer warriors had been divinely gathered on her behalf. Before Lisa could even read the results, Rhonda bolted into the bathroom. Hugging and crying, the two sisters were amazed at God's wonderful news—the results were positive! A miracle baby was about to make its way into this world, and Lisa was going to be a mother!

Overjoyed, stunned and somewhat in shock, Lisa headed home to share this miracle with her husband. Rhonda ran upstairs to her husband Danny. She announced the miracle to him. Then he shared how the Lord had prompted him to pray for Lisa at that very time.

Soon Rhonda called me at work to share the good news. I shared with her how the Lord had prompted me to pray at 11:00 A.M. Rhonda announced that was the exact time of Lisa's pregnancy test.

As the day went on, Rhonda learned, across the region, God had dropped the spontaneous desire into hearts to pray fervently for one particular woman and her name was Lisa.

Almost twenty-four hours to the minute since Rhonda's first request for prayer, the Lord had given his awesome and wonderful answer.

Lisa's heart must be singing praises similar to those voiced by Hannah. "My heart rejoices in the Lord! Oh, how the Lord has blessed me! Oh how the Lord has blessed me!"

Calling Out Your Name

Jim Cymbala

Calvin Hunt met the trim, attractive Miriam and her two preschoolers when he was just twenty years old. Miriam lived in the apartment two floors below his mother and she and Calvin warmed to each other right away. Little Monique and Freddy liked the handsome young construction worker with the hard hat who made them laugh. Calvin was also something of a weekend musician, playing guitar and singing in nightclubs.

Miriam's divorce was not yet final and Calvin had to comfort her more than once after she had been beaten up by her estranged husband. On one occasion, when her husband knocked her out cold, Calvin took Miriam to the Emergency Room. Their relationship flourished over the next year and then even survived a one-year Army stint by Calvin that took him away from New York City.

"When I came back home," Calvin admits, "the easiest thing for me to do was just to move in with her. I went back to working road construction, and we had enough money to party through the weekends." The couple eventually added snorting cocaine to their fairly heavy drinking as they and their friends sought new thrills. Then they added marijuana to the mix, sometimes even sprinkling the joints with cocaine before rolling them in order to experience both drugs at once.

The live-in arrangement continued with little change, until five years later when Miriam told Calvin they ought to get married. And so in 1984, they wed.

One night the best man from their wedding invited them to a party at his home that featured something new: "free-basing" cocaine or heating it and smoking it through a glass bottle. Calvin was intrigued; he asked his friend for a hit. But the new drug didn't seem to have much effect, Calvin thought. Miriam gave it a try as well, with minimal results. Or so they thought. Not until they left the friend's apartment at 7:30 the next morning, having been awake all night and having spent Calvin's entire $720 paycheck for the week, did they realize they had discovered something powerfully attractive—and deadly. They had now joined the world of crack cocaine.

"I remember us going back home and I just felt horrible the whole weekend," Calvin says. "By the time I went to work on Monday, I was lecturing myself about being more responsible. I had a family to support, and I needed to get back in control.

"Would you believe that by the next Friday night when I cashed my check, I called Miriam and told her to get the kids ready for bed early because I'd be bringing home 'the stuff'? I showed up with all the new paraphernalia, ready for action. I prepared the crack over the kitchen stove just as I had seen my friend do it the week before, and again the two of us were up all night. By the time the sun came up Saturday morning, we had gone through another whole paycheck."

This pattern endured for eight months. Meanwhile, household bills went unpaid, the children lacked warm winter clothing, and the rent fell behind. Miriam's brothers, who were Christians, urged her to stop destroying herself, but neither she nor Calvin would listen.

Calvin's obsession with drugs grew ever stronger, and not just on the weekends. If he had any spare cash in his pocket, it went for crack. If he didn't have cash, he would manufacture some by stealing the tires or the battery from a parked car to resell. Some nights he didn't come home at all.

Obviously Calvin's job performance suffered. One day his boss called Calvin aside for a talk. There were tears in the man's eyes as he said quietly, "You've been one of my most valued employees. I don't know what's happening, and I don't want to know—but whatever it is, you better get it fixed, because you're about to lose your job."

The truth was, Calvin had a new super boss in his life: crack. "I began losing a lot of weight," Calvin says. "I'd be gone three, four, even five days at a time—spending my life in crack dens. Yes, I had a home and a wife and two children—but when I was doing crack, home was the last place I wanted to be.

"The people I did drugs with were actually a pretty scary bunch—violent and heartless. But as long as I was high, I didn't even notice that."

Miriam grew increasingly concerned. What was happening to the man she loved, her one-time knight in shining armor? Hadn't she already been through enough chaos with her first husband— and now this?

One night she looked at her two children sleeping innocently in bed while Calvin and his friends were in the kitchen getting high. Moral principles once learned long ago seemed to rise up to warn her of where this was all heading. She promptly threw all the guys out—including Calvin.

Miriam began to see that she was being terribly betrayed by a man for the second time in her life. The first one had beaten her physically; the second one was hurting her and her children even more painfully with his addiction. Like Judah of old, he was wreaking tremendous damage on his family through his unbridled thrill-seeking.

"I pleaded with him to stop," says Miriam. I said, "Calvin, this is going to kill us! It's going to destroy our marriage." The arguments got so bad that sometimes I had to have him escorted out of the house. My son began studying ways to add more locks to the apartment so Calvin couldn't get back in.

At the very time Calvin was deserting the family, Miriam put her faith in Christ. Her spiritual life deepened, and her prayer life increased. She found a church and would openly ask for the prayers of others to bring her husband back from the brink. She refused to contemplate the other options: separation, divorce, and his untimely death. She simply believed that God would somehow rescue their family.

She even began to tell Calvin, "God is going to set you free— I just know it!" Of course, that made him furious. He also got irked at the Brooklyn Tabernacle Choir as they began to sing. She loved it and would respond in worship, sometimes even weeping for joy as she praised the Lord. Calvin would snap back, "If that stuff makes you cry, why don't you turn it off?" He would sometimes fling the cassette out the window, but his wife would quickly replace it.

One day young Monique found a flyer announcing a Friday night showing of the film *A Cry for Freedom,* being sponsored by Christ Tabernacle in Queens. The twelve-year-old insisted that Dad go with them to see it. He brushed her off.

Suddenly something rose up within the girl. She said, "Daddy, remember all the neat things we used to do together? We don't do anything anymore. You know what—it's all about you and that drug, whatever it is! Your problem is, you're hooked and you won't admit it!"

Calvin flared back. "You shut up! Keep talking like that and I'll give you a whipping!"

"Go ahead, Daddy!" the brave girl responded. "You can beat

me and stomp on me if you want—but when you're finished, you'll still be hooked on that stuff." At that, she ran out of the kitchen.

Calvin picked up the flyer from the table. He looked at the sketch of a man inside the bottle that is used for smoking crack, his hands pressed against the glass with a desperate look on his face. Calvin's heart melted enough that he reluctantly agreed to attend the showing.

At the last minute, Calvin tried to back out, but without success. The film's story line turned out to be a shockingly close replica of the Hunts themselves: a husband addicted to crack, and his formerly addicted wife now praying for his deliverance. When the pastor gave an invitation at the end, Calvin was the first one kneeling at the altar. "I didn't actually ask Jesus to come into my heart," he says, "But I was just so guilt-ridden that I had to at least pray and admit the pain I was causing everyone. I started to cry. Miriam and the kids came alongside, and we all cried together."

The next Sunday, the family returned to church, and while Miriam and the children were overjoyed, Calvin still was not willing to get serious about the Lord. *God can't do anything for me,* he told himself. *What am I doing here?* By the next weekend. He was on the run again.

Now the church body began to pray harder for Calvin Hunt's salvation. Calvin learned to time his visits back to the apartment during the hours when he knew everyone would be at church. He would sneak in to get a fresh supply of clean clothes and then quickly leave.

I knew that Calvin was in a prison," says Miriam. "Being an ex-addict myself—I had done heroin before I ever met him—I knew the unbelievable power of this kind of substance. That's why I prayed so hard, crying out to God to set him free, and got all my friends to pray with me. Every mealtime prayer with my kids, every bedtime prayer included, 'O God, please set Daddy free!'"

Another three years went by. Calvin got worse instead of better. At one point he was actually sleeping in a large doghouse in someone's backyard rather than going home to his own bed. He was seriously dehydrated, his cheeks sunken, giving him the wasted look so common among addicts. With no money, Miriam and the children had to apply for food stamps and Medicaid.

Finally, one night—the same night as Christ Tabernacle's weekly prayer meeting—Calvin headed once again for the family apartment after his wife and children had left. In the quietness he found some food in the refrigerator, then took a shower and put on clean clothes. There was still time for a short nap, so he decided to lie down.

But for some reason, he couldn't sleep. Soon he heard a noise. From a closet came the soft sound of someone weeping! He sat up. Maybe Miriam and the children were home after all.

He looked in the children's rooms, under the beds, inside the various closets. No one! But the sobbing continued. He stood in the living room and said out loud, "I know you guys are in here—come on out!" Nobody appeared.

Now Calvin was spooked. He thought of lying down once again, but something inside him seemed to say, *If you go to sleep tonight, you'll never wake up again.* He panicked. Running out the door, he dashed three blocks to the church to see if his wife and children were really at the prayer meeting or not.

He burst into the church and stood at the back of the center aisle, scanning the crowd. Suddenly the same sounds of crying struck his ears—only much louder than back in the apartment. The whole congregation was in earnest prayer, calling out *his* name to God in faith! Calvin was thunderstruck as he slowly moved down the aisle, gazing at the people's upraised hands and their eyes tightly shut in prayer, tears running down their faces. "O God, wherever Calvin Hunt is, bring him to this building!" they pleaded. "Don't let this family go through this horror another day. Lord, you are able! Set him free from his bondage once and for all!"

Soon Calvin found himself at the front, directly before the pulpit. The pastor in charge opened his eyes, took one glance—and then gazed upward toward heaven as he said into the microphone, "Thank you, Lord! Thank you, Jesus! Here he is!"

With that, the congregation went absolutely crazy. They had been calling upon the Lord to bring Calvin to himself, and it was happening right before their very eyes.

Falling to his knees, Calvin burst into uncontrollable sobs. Miriam and the children came from their pew to huddle around him as he prayed, "O God, I've become everything I said I'd never be. I don't want to die this way. Please come into my life and set me free. Oh, Jesus, I need you so much!"

That summer night in 1988 was the turning point for Calvin Hunt, says Miriam. "It was almost as if he had walked slowly down the center aisle of the church as in a wedding, to be married to Christ. Jesus was patiently waiting for him at the altar. No wonder we all burst into tears!"

A Jail Chaplain's Meditation

Lorette Piper

Sitting in our circle one night in the juvenile jail, Mark, a seventeen-year-old African American, told us he was leaving soon, going home to face his enemies. He told me that he had done everything I suggested for one whole year, and still he found no God. And, he added, if there were a God, what kind of God would have set him up to live the kind of life he had lived so far? Mark's parents had deserted him and his five siblings. Then, year after year, they had been abused in foster homes.

Exhausted and overwhelmed as I was that night, I began a ferocious inner dialogue with God? "Mark is right! It's too hard for him and for all of us! Where are You? We need more help! Show us Your love! Do something, say something! This is a showdown, right here and right now." I crossed my arms, and we waited in silence. And waited.

Suddenly, up leapt a sixteen-year-old Hispanic boy who planted himself, with hands clenched and biceps bulging, in front of Mark. I said to You, "How could You add injury to insult? Now I'll have to use the red phone. There's going to be a fight."

But Jorge was simply positioning himself to speak urgently and formally to Mark. "Mark, I know there is a God because every night I stand and pray at my cell window and I look at the stars and I feel God's love for me as the tears are running down my cheeks. And Mark, I know there's a God because...I know there's a God

"Because...I love you!"

And I felt Your laughter in my heart, and I heard Your words echoing in my mind: "For God is greater than our hearts and knows all things.... Beloved, let us love one another, because love is from God: Everyone who loves is born of God and knows God.... We love because God first loves us.... For God is greater than our hearts and knows all things."

Once again You reminded me that my job is not Your job, that when I step back, You step in, and that the mystery of love at the center of our lives is radically near and radically other.

Me, Lead a Prayer Group?

Claire Donch

Some years ago my husband Mike and I were in deep financial trouble. We had a lot of bills to pay, especially my medical ones, and things had gotten so bad we were forced to accept food from my church and money from the local Christmas fund to buy our little girl, Heidi, a winter coat.

We weren't the only ones. We live in Erie, Pennsylvania, a town of 120,000. In spite of the corporate presence in Erie of General Electric, Hammermill Paper, and Bucyrus-Erie, the unemployment rate was eighteen per cent! Mike worked for a cable TV company on commission; he received no regular salary, and though he was working more than fifty hours a week, his paychecks continually dwindled. So on weekends, he worked as a saxophonist with a band, and I had a part-time job. But still, with the steady drain of a big medical bill and several other unexpected setbacks, we couldn't make it. Our problem was not *un*employment but *under*employment.

The day I returned from shopping for Heidi's coat, Mike came home for lunch with his co-worker, Randy Weed. Randy enjoyed eating at our house; soup and sandwiches were a break from the macaroni-and-cheese he and his family were subsisting on. Mike had had a bad morning. Out of twenty-five calls, not one person had subscribed to the cable system. And while Mike was on his home-visiting rounds, one guy had actually thrown him off a porch.

I was heartsick as I made the sandwiches. As humiliating as it was accepting charity, at least we had been able to get Heidi's present. But it would be a slim Christmas at Randy's house. All at once I felt like crying—for us, for Randy's kids, for all the decent, hard-working families struggling in the recession that gripped the nation.

A few days after the shopping expedition, an issue of *Guideposts* arrived. One of the articles in that issue grabbed me. Titled "The Park Ridge, New Jersey Experiment," it was about Robert Miller, a Christian businessman who started a prayer group with unemployed friends. I wondered if this sort of group could work for Mike, because the Experiment story told how good things began to happen for Bob Miller and his friends as they prayed together about their common problems. Most of them found jobs; all were strengthened and comforted.

When Mike got home that night I asked him to read the Miller story. He didn't want to at first. Mike, who's a church-going Catholic, believed that *Guideposts* was for—and about—Protestants. I persisted and Mike finally read Bob Miller's story.

Initially he wasn't impressed. But the next day he went back and read the story again. A nagging feeling told him he had missed something; it was that Bob Miller, too, was Roman Catholic. And Mike related to the problems of the men in the story. True, he had a job, but the financial stresses were the same.

I was surprised when Mike suggested that we write for guidelines. Soon we received a letter back, with suggestions for starting a prayer group. We found that the basic idea of the Experiment is that partners pray for thirty days, seeking answers to each other's problems. The guidelines suggested that newcomers start small by praying with a single partner. So Mike—who'd always been unwilling to pray aloud, even with me—asked Randy if he would pray with him. I called up my minister's wife, Judy Schmidt, and asked her if she'd try the Experiment with me. Both agreed.

We began our prayer experiment in earnest. We knew, though, that we couldn't just pray and then sit, waiting for something to drop out of the blue. The cable TV job, for instance, was not going to improve; prayer helped Mike face that harsh fact. And so, though he had always hated job-hunting, he now attacked the want-ads with enthusiasm.

Thirty days went by and at that point Mike and Randy were so encouraged that they got some friends together and began a prayer group. If anybody had told me six months earlier that these rough, tough former cocktail-lounge musicians would be praying together, I would have laughed. But there they were, with bowed heads, talking to God about one another's hurts and needs.

A week after starting his prayer group, Mike was called in for an interview with a top national insurance company. The job was just what he had been hoping for.

While Mike waited for an offer, he was optimistic and full of faith. But I was more anxious and frightened than ever. Despite the fact that Judy and I were praying together, I was calling her two and three times a day, trying to cope with my feelings, because *I* was the one facing the bill collectors; *I* was the one wrestling with a tight budget, trying to feed our family on next to nothing, caring for Heidi and running our home.

I began to think: *We wives bear burdens with our men, and we encourage them. But who helps us bear our burdens, who encourages us? Where do we get support?* Suddenly an all-too-obvious idea popped into my head: *Why not start a prayer group for wives?*

I asked Mike what he thought about my forming a group. "Sure," he replied. "You can do it, Claire." But then I hesitated, asking myself, *Am I really capable?* I've had a high-frequency hearing loss since birth, and I often rely on lip-reading. Because of this, when I become nervous, my speech tends to get garbled. My previously strong faith was wavering at this point, so how could I hope to lead a prayer group?

"Mike, suppose I make a mistake, forget what to say?"

"So what? Wing it." He wasn't letting me off the hook.

"I'm not a leader," I protested.

"Honey, we salesmen have a saying: 'You have nothing to lose and everything to gain, so pick up the phone and dial.'"

So that's what I did. I knew Judy would join the group. Who else? Linda Webber was a minister's daughter... she wouldn't think I was a religious fanatic.

Linda was supportive. Even though she had three part-time jobs and a young son, she found the time to give the group a try. With two positive responses, I got the courage to dial seven more numbers. One more person accepted.

I read and reread the guidelines until I had memorized them. The first meeting of our women's prayer group was held at our home. There were four of us: three Protestants and a Catholic. I opened with a very short prayer, asking God to be with us. My voice had a wobble I hoped wasn't too noticeable. Then, silence. I took a deep breath.

"Judy and I have been praying for more than thirty days now," I began. "We feel a need to support each other. Now, with this group, we believe we all can help one another by talking and praying about what is bothering us in our lives. Please don't feel you have to contribute if it makes you uncomfortable. But I'll tell you what's happened in my life..."

Then, as simply as I could, I told my friends for the first time of the terrible pressures Mike and I had been facing. "But you know," I said, "Judy and I have kept a log. At the beginning of our Thirty-Day Experiment, it was filled with negative thoughts. Toward the end, most of our entries were positive. I feel better about things, and I think Judy does too.

"The concept in the guidelines that encourages me to create a women's group is this: *God will accept you at any level of faith.* If He can believe that self-conscious, sometimes tongue-tied Claire Donch can accomplish something, then I can believe it too! Think about it."

One of the other women spoke up. "Well, I'm not much good at praying aloud, but I need help. My husband is underemployed...just like Mike. And I'm having an awful time handling our three kids... You know, my oldest, Joey is only three. I need more patience...." She stopped, suddenly embarrassed. Judy patted her hand in encouragement.

The other women began to open up about the things that were troubling them. Judy admitted she and her husband were having financial problems involving the sale of their home in New York City. Without the proceeds from a sale, they struggled to meet their current bills. She asked for prayer.

All at once I realized I had forgotten to be afraid! Instead, there was a beautiful feeling of caring in the room. And something even more wonderful—the presence of the Lord. He was there with us as we talked and prayed. The words of St. Paul came to me: "Bear ye one another's burdens, and so fulfill the law of Christ" (Galatians 6:2). And that "law" is simply to love one another. That was what we were doing. And that was why we felt Him there with us!

Before we closed with The Lord's Prayer, we agreed to pray for one another every day.

We decided to hold weekly meetings—and almost immediately

we ran into problems with the husbands. Our meeting was scheduled at 8:00 P.M., just when one of the fellows was expecting his dinner. Another husband didn't fancy himself as a babysitter. But eventually we worked out our problems and have stuck to our schedule.

Since we began last spring, our women's prayer group has gained some new members: others have dropped out. We're a small group; we think the Lord wants it that way until we're a little more experienced.

All of us have financial and related problems. One new member works part-time to help ends meet. Her particular problem is that her husband has had to take a job in a distant city. Like many of us, she had taken on chores ordinarily done by her husband— having the car serviced and mowing the lawn. When her husband comes home weekends, she tries to avoid burdening him with problems, so she finds the support of the group indispensable. However, she has been concerned about managing her time better. She has asked the group to pray about it.

So it goes, week by week. When one set of problems is resolved, there are always new ones to share and pray over.

Why has our women's group thrived? I think it's because we're "other-directed." When you stop to think of it, married women with children to raise can become isolated and self-absorbed. We get caught up in our family's problems; we're starved for interaction with other adults.

So the prayer group gets us out of the house and out of ourselves. We realize in a deep way that we are not alone in our problems. Not all of us can attend every meeting. Sometimes there are only two of us. But it doesn't matter. Jesus himself said: "For where two of three are gathered together in my name, there am I in the midst of them" (Matthew 18:20).

And what about my husband and me? Well, before we joined

the group, Mike and I were, in a sense, leading separate spiritual lives. Now we're closer than ever. We have a new respect for each other's beliefs. We concentrate on our unity in Christ, not on the differences. And, oh yes, Mike *was* offered a job by the insurance company; he accepted and is now happier in his work.

Are you facing problems? Are you scared, unsure? You *can't* be more afraid than this scaredy-cat was! And if I could step out in faith, anyone can. Let me tell you—prayer works. It works wonders. But you may never know, if you don't try it.

CHAPTER 5

For surely I know the plans I have for you,

says the Lord, plans for your welfare

and not for harm,

to give you a future with hope.

Then when you call upon me

and come and pray to me,

I will hear you.

JEREMIAH 29:11-12 *(NRSV)*

God Knows Our Needs

Lord, You know my need.

Your hand is on my life.

Help me not forget

to trust You.

MARILYN WINEGARDNER

When Your Prayers Seem Unanswered

Constance Foster

What are we to conclude when we have prayed for a long time and nothing seems to be any different from before? Is God whimsical, given to listening to one person but turning a deaf ear on another, or hearing us on some occasions and ignoring us on others? Many people ask themselves these questions. When they pray and things remain much the same or even grow worse, they may come to the conclusion that prayer is at best uncertain, and at worst futile.

I became so much interested in this subject of apparently unanswered prayer that for several years now I have been gathering records of such instances.

Carol W. was a young college student when she first came to my attention. In spite of hard work and great ambition, Carol was failing to make passing grades in certain subjects and had been warned that unless she did well on her term examinations, she would be dropped at the end of the year. Carol was praying sincerely for success in her exams. But a month later she phoned me and her first words were, "Well, I prayed but nothing happened."

Carol had flunked two courses and the college dropped her. Certainly surface appearances here would seem to justify her conclusion that "nothing happened" as the result of prayer. But wait! And never forget that God knows more than we do about what is for our highest good.

A few weeks after she returned home, Carol consulted a psychologist who was an expert at determining in what areas an individual's best talents lay. He gave her a battery of aptitude tests that revealed she was extremely gifted in spatial perception and mechanical ability. They also showed that she was not naturally a good student where abstract subjects, such as she had taken at college, were concerned.

Carol took a course at a technical school in x-ray therapy and medical techniques. Today she is head of a large hospital laboratory with a dozen assistants under her direction, making a splendid salary and happy in her work. Did nothing happen when she prayed? Graduation from a liberal arts college was not the right answer to her needs and abilities. Carol didn't know it. But God did.

Now let us turn to another example of apparently unanswered prayer. It concerns an elderly widow whose husband's death had left her almost destitute and in danger of losing her large home. She could no longer meet the heavy expense of maintaining it. Mrs. Horton wrote me for prayers that she might be able by some miracle to keep it, together with all her cherished possessions. A few months later, another letter from her reached me. "We both prayed," she wrote, "But nothing happened." The house was to be sold at auction the following week. Mrs. Horton was heartbroken.

During the next few days, Mrs. Horton went through her house with tear-stained eyes, sorting and discarding the accumulation of long years of living in it. In the attic she ran across an old stamp collection that had been in her husband's family for years. She almost threw it in the pile of rubbish. Of what use were a lot of old stamps? But something made her put it aside to save.

A year went by before she thought of it again. The house had been sold. "Nothing had happened." She was bitter. Her prayer had not been answered. Then one day she happened to see an advertisement in a large city newspaper, listing the value of certain rare stamps. Mrs. Horton made a special trip to see the dealer, carrying the old collection with her. When she left his office, she was dazed and unbelieving, for in her purse she had his check for nearly $11,000!

The big old house had been much too large for one woman to care for comfortably. She did not need all that space. Today, she realizes it. What she required was smaller living quarters together with enough money in the bank for her expenses. That is exactly what God gave her in answer to her supposedly "unanswered" prayer.

Then there was the businessman who had been praying for an increase in salary. Instead, his company reshuffled its personnel and he was placed in a different department with a pay *decrease.* They told him he could leave if he was not satisfied to stay on at the lower figure.

He phoned me about the new development and his voice was bitter, "What good is prayer?" he demanded. This is just another variation on the "But nothing happened" theme. Where was God in all this, he wanted to know. Where indeed? Right where He always is, of course, busy making all things work together for good in our individual lives. Had nothing happened?

It seems that my friend had never before been engaged in selling but the new job gave him a chance to try his hand at it and he proved to have a genius for it. Today, three years later, he is sales manager for his firm at a salary five times larger than the one he was receiving when he first prayed for an increase. More important still, he is doing work that is productive and rewarding. Had he not been "demoted," the promotion could never have happened.

My final story concerns a very dear neighbor whose retarded child could not seem to learn. Betty came to me in great distress one day. "It's the last straw," she burst. "As if I didn't already have enough grief and trouble with poor little Karen, now I have to take in my husband's father. He's practically senile. Oh please pray as you've never prayed before that we can get some other relative to take care of him."

But there was no other relative able to take in the old man. The day Grandpa arrived, my neighbor echoed the same old sad refrain, "We prayed, but nothing happened. I'm stuck." Nothing happened? It looked that way, didn't it? But God had something wonderful in store for that mother. He had the highest welfare of her retarded child at heart. For tiny Karen began to blossom in Grandpa's company. They seemed to understand each other and soon they were inseparable. Grandpa was not critical of her failings and never pushed her beyond her capacity. He accepted and loved her as she was and for herself alone.

For hours on end Karen sat in Grandpa's lap while he rocked and sang to her. She began to talk and laugh and play. Today, she is a practically normal child and although the old man now is no longer living, the family is eternally grateful that God brought him to stay with them and love Karen into overcoming her handicap.

Make no mistake. There is no such thing as an unanswered prayer. God hears every whisper of our hearts but He loves us too much always to answer in the precise terms that we ask. He often has a better answer.

So never say, "But nothing happened" when your prayers are not immediately fulfilled as you think they should be. Something always happens. A spiritual force has been set in motion that never stops vibrating in the universal atmosphere. A great chain reaction takes place, which may not bring you exactly what you asked for, perhaps, but something infinitely better for your eternal advantage. In short, it is impossible for you to pray and then be able to say truthfully, "But nothing happened."

We Walk by Faith

Toni Grayson

I had just returned to California after burying Nana, my ninety-seven-year-old grandmother. I had endured the loss of relatives before, but this was an unusually painful period in my life. While on "death watch," my grandmother asked me to not let her die. As I looked at her lying helpless in that bed, I prayed to God for the right words to say. As intensely as I had prayed, I heard myself saying to her, "You have to talk to Jesus, Nana." The next morning, when I returned to the nursing home, Nana softly told me she was ready to die.

I returned to Los Angeles to face the notice that my job had ended. To make matters worse, my seventeen-year-old car named "Lulu" died in the driveway, after allowing me to run some errands that included picking up the Sunday paper. That night, not knowing which way to turn, I fell on my knees and uttered those four simple but powerful words, "God, please help me." Just then, the telephone rang. My friend Julie called to ask if there was anything she could do for me. I explained that my car had also "died" and, without a job, it would be impossible to get financing for a car. Then it happened. Julie asked me if I had heard about the public car auctions advertised in the Sunday paper. As I turned to the classifieds, something inside of me said, "Go charge a car!" When I told Julie what I wanted to do, she agreed to pick me up in the morning, attend church service, and then go to the auction.

We prayed for God's guidance and wisdom to purchase a car *if it be His will.*

Attending church prevented us from getting to the auction in time to inspect the cars prior to the bidding. So, without the benefit of knowing what was to be sold, Julie and I sat in quiet anticipation as various cars came before the crowd to be sold. Then there appeared this beautiful black vehicle that was the same model as Lulu. As they drove her into the arena, Julie unexpectedly elbowed me to bid. Without hesitation, my hand sprang up and, in what seemed only a few seconds later, the auctioneer yelled out, "Sold." I had won the bid for the exact amount my credit card would allow! I was ecstatic yet fearful. I had bought this car virtuously sight unseen. Did it even have a back seat? Did the lights/windshield wipers work? What about the engine? As we stood waiting for the care, I looked to heaven and thought, *Dear God, have I truly lost my mind?*

Just then, I heard the humming sound of a familiar engine. As I watched this black machine being driven toward me, my eyes were drawn to the front license plate. There, inscribed in big bold black calligraphy letters between a design of two palm trees was the name, "JESUS!" Now, perhaps the previous owner put this plate on the car because his name was Jesus (later I found out the car had come from Florida) or perhaps the owner was also a Christian. Whatever the reason, I choose to believe that the plate was a message from God (and my grandmother) that all is well; and a sense of peace came over me.

It's been two years since I purchased "Lulu Two" (as I call her) and she is doing fine. I use the car not only for personal needs but to transport God's people when in need. Always during the ride, I tell them the story of how I walked by faith.

The Other Side of the Tracks

Paula Spencer

I am sitting in the silence of my attic study, enjoying the summer evening with the windows wide open, a cautious luxury I afford myself only on the second story our of house. Suddenly, out in the night, I hear a series of gunshots, then a frightening pause, then another series. The shots are coming from the block behind our house. I open the window and peer into the now-quiet darkness. I notice a basket in the yard, left by my children as they collected flowers and leaves earlier in the day. An old blue sedan moves by, the only car around.

I find Chris in our bedroom, unaware of the gunshots because of our noisy air conditioner. I tell him what I've heard. We walk downstairs to look out our back door. We both know that the drug corner that used to be three blocks away is now on the next block over, since they moved everybody out of the housing project that's slated for destruction. We stand outside, listening. A light flashes on the next block. Random voices scatter through the air. We decide to go back in.

What would you do if your husband came home one day and asked you to move from your comfortable home on four suburban acres to a poor, crime-studded, inner-city neighborhood? Mary Lawrence Woodhull cried.

She wasn't entirely surprised by the suggestion, though. More than a year earlier, her husband Chris cofounded Tribe One, a nonprofit ministry in Knoxville, Tennessee, dedicated to keeping kids out of gangs. Mostly impoverished African Americans, these young people inevitably tend to spiral toward one of two fates: jail or death. And they live, of course, in the city. The best way to fully understand and reach them is to live among them—as is true of missionary work anywhere.

"When Chris talked about moving into the city, my blood ran backward and got chilly," says Lawrence (who goes by her middle name), thirty-eight, who shares the bone structure and elegant simplicity of a young Sissy Spacek. "I said, 'No. I'm not made that way. I can't do it.'"

Chris persisted, and every time he broached the subject, an argument followed. "He *so* wanted to move there and I *so much* didn't. The more we argued, the more polarized we became," Lawrence says. "Finally, he said, "OK. I'm not going to bring it up anymore. If you want to move, let me know."

At first she was relieved. But to her surprise, when Chris backed off from his *yes* position, she was able to creep away from her knee-jerk "no." *What if we did move?* She made lists of pros and cons. She prayed. Ultimately, her decision boiled down to this: Chris could only pursue his work in the inner city. She could pursue her work—caring for a family—anywhere.

As it was, Chris was gone from 7:00 A.M. to 6:00 P.M., oftentimes longer. Perhaps if they were all living the same life, she reasoned, their family bonds could grow even stronger. Chris began showing her houses in the inner city and, as Lawrence says, "That would put the nail in the coffin on the idea. He showed me one place next to the interstate, and I cried all the way home."

Another day, they saw a seven-gabled, 108-year-old Victorian with, as the real estate agents say, *potential.* It wasn't for sale. "Want to make an offer?" the owner asked anyway. Lawrence declined. She wasn't that ready.

Around this same time, Lawrence overheard some restaurant customers talking about the spiritual musical *Christy* which was playing in a nearby town in the Smoky Mountains. Intrigued, she went to see it herself—twice in one week. She so loved the plucky heroine's story that she then read Catherine Marshall's novel of the same name. Soon after, in another coincidence, she learned the book was a beloved grandmother's favorite. "In the book, I saw Christy choose between a life of tea parties in Asheville, North Carolina, and a life among the impoverished Appalachian people," she explains. "Something clicked inside me and I became convinced God was trying to tell me something— that I had a choice between comfort and safety or adventure and trust in whatever journey he might provide."

I return to my desk, but I'm drawn to the window again. This time I can see the lights of an emergency vehicle bouncing off my daughters' baskets in the yard. Then I hear a commotion and sirens. Chris and I return to our listening post. We hear a woman shouting. More shouting. I am thinking, "Wouldn't that mean someone is hurt because it is a red and white light like an ambulance and not a blue and white light like a police car." I get goose bumps as I finish my thought. Someone is hurt. We stand there in the darkness silently shrugging at one another. Finally, we hold hands and Chris prays for whoever is struggling for life one block over.

Back inside, Chris looks at me. I already know what he's going to say. And he thinks he knows how I am going to respond. Reluctantly, with dread, he asks me the expected question: "Does this make you afraid?"

Lawrence Arnett was a successful, driven art director at a

media company when she and her husband first met. Chris Woodhull was a quiet, literary fellow with a debonair Ralph Lauren wardrobe who worked in the company's research department. "Once I peeked in his closet, and I swear I'd never seen so many Polo shirts in one place outside of a store," she says, laughing.

They married in August, 1986. Lawrence, more career-oriented, continued to put in fifty-and sixty-hour weeks, often traveling for business. Bored with research, Chris considered pursuing a master's degree to teach writing. Together they spent a lot of money on movies, restaurant meals, and dry cleaning.

A year after their wedding, Chris' growing interest in African American literature, jazz and culture led him to take a job as a youth director for an urban-aid nonprofit ministry. He tutored, directed after-school programs and also raised funds for his salary. "My mother was horrified," recalls Lawrence, who grew up in an "old-money" part of town and whose businessman father had been once named Knoxville's Man of the Year. "She didn't like the idea that [Chris'] job included raising money."

For Lawrence, though, it made sense. "I once heard the designer Milton Glaser say that the best design feels inevitable. And that's how this felt."

However, as her husband's professional enthusiasm grew, Lawrence's plummeted. Fulfilling projects had been drying up at work. She felt burned out. Then her first pregnancy ended in a miscarriage. "My soul felt stomped on," she says. "So I quit."

She got pregnant again immediately, and in 1991 delivered a baby girl named Tess. Baby sister Paris followed three years later. At first, the family lived off the generous severance Lawrence received (the company had been seeking volunteers for a downsizing when she decided to leave). "Then we just realized that we could live on two-thirds less income just fine," she says. For one thing, she didn't feel a need to treat herself to meals out and shopping sprees as compensation for the job stress.

Instead, Lawrence focused on family. And she watched Chris and his partner, Danny Mayfield (who, in 1998, became Knoxville's only twenty-something African American city councilman), grow more passionate about their mission: showing a better way to young, prospective gang members who lived twenty miles—and another world—away from the Woodhull's wooded acreage.

Does hearing gunfire in the middle of the night make me afraid? I answer in a way that surprises my husband. Two years ago, I would have been terrified. But I'm not anymore. I understand now that those young men on the street are not likely to bother me since I do not buy drugs. I probably know half of them by sight. Some of them have had pancakes with lots of syrup at our house. I answer Chris: "I'm not scared. I'm just glad you and Danny want to reach these guys." Who else is going to love them? On the way back to my attic desk, I stop and kiss both of my sleeping children—just as those boys might have been kissed by their mamas once upon a time.

When friends and relatives heard Chris and Lawrence were contemplating a move to the inner city, not one person agreed with them. Even their handful of ministry friends who already lived there urged them to think twice about leaving their lovely home. "So the choice had to be made only with God's help," she says. "I saw that God was offering Chris and me a chance to be held in the palm of his hand. His protection would no longer be a gentle hope; it would be a necessity."

By coincidence or fate, the old Victorian house they'd liked was still available a full year after they'd first seen it. Three days before they closed the sale, Lawrence's mother burst into tears at the sight of the place; it was filthy and strewn with old pizza boxes by the last occupants—five frat boys. She asked Lawrence how she could put her children in such jeopardy. Mother and daughter exchanged heated words. "Going through the closing without having my mom's support was the worst," Lawrence recalls, "Like getting married without your mom's blessing."

On a gray, muddy January day in 1996—sobbing with apprehension and praying all the way—she drove to the house to meet a friend who had volunteered to help clean and paint. To her joy and amazement, standing next to the friend was Lawrence's mom, covered in dirt. "I don't support you, but I'm not going to give up on you," she said.

"It has been a hard adjustment," Lawrence acknowledges. Hard to take time away from her daughters to make the house habitable. Hard that the girls, now ages seven and four, cannot safely play in the yard unsupervised. Hard to see your old family rocking chairs, the ones you'd painted a cheerful red and set up next to a checkerboard for the neighborhood kids, stolen off your front porch. Hard to get used to beggars and people trying to sell you a loaf of bread that they just got from the food kitchen down the street. Hard to find a drunk lurching at your front door. Hard to get used to the occasional sounds of gunfire.

When they discovered the house needed a new roof—a $10,000 job, thanks to all those gables—Lawrence panicked. "I thought maybe it was a sign that we shouldn't have come here, that I had misread everything else."

Living solely on Chris' ministry salary means being supported entirely by donations. One memorable paycheck came to sixty-five dollars, though the usual take is enough for the family to live comfortably on a firm budget, Lawrence says.

But the hardships have been balanced by light. The family is closer than ever, she says. Chris, who is based in a home office, comes in and out all day. "He's more available to [our kids] now."

She says. "In fact, they sometimes call me Daddy and him Mommy, which sounds wonderful."

Lawrence says she's made more friends, real go-to-the-mat-for-you friends, in the city than she did when isolated in the suburbs. She and Pam Mader, a close friend, obtained a grant from a local church to start a Montessori-based Christian education program for area three-to-six-year-olds under the umbrella of Tribe One. They call it The Manger ("because Jesus was born in poverty, not in a fancy house in Jerusalem").

Although the Woodhulls are active in their local community, Lawrence did not enroll Tess in the local elementary school which has some of the poorest test scores in the city. She home-schools Tess, while Paris attends a preschool in a nearby suburb where Lawrence teaches classes in art part-time. "Just because we're here does not mean I'm going to completely put that agenda on my children." She says. "But my children do know what a poor person looks like, what a homeless person looks like. I'm glad they are meeting people different from us, because it's a big world. There are also things I wish they hadn't seen, like the drunken man in front of our home who the police had to wrestle to the ground. Those things hurt me," she says. "But I knew my kids needed their daddy, and that we would not be a family until we were fixed on a common vision."

Lawrence worries about her daughters, but is quick to remind herself that she'd be second-guessing her choices wherever she lived. *What parents can guarantee who their children will become?* We won't know for years how our decision has affected our children, what seeds we've planted. I hope that the trade-offs will be there, that life will be richer for them because of the experience.

"Sure there have been a lot of hard things, but there are also things that I would have missed if we hadn't moved here," she adds. "I once heard someone say that you can ride the merry-go-round at the fair, or go up and down with the roller coaster." I've always been a merry-go-round kind of person. But the roller coaster is much more interesting."

It somehow feels urgent to get these words on paper. As I finish, something in the room catches my eye. The window is reflecting the red image of the neon cross of a church. I think back to our first night here in the community. Our daughter, Tess, four at the time, pointed at that cross and said, "Come look, Mommy. Jesus lives in our neighborhood." And tonight, somehow, despite evidence to the contrary, I am sure he is here with us.

That night, four young men were shot.

God's Matrimonial Service

Albert Gilbert

I was fifty years old and feeling discouraged because I hadn't met the "right lady." I prayed for a wife, but nothing seemed to come of it.

Then, in March 1991, I read a story that told of a fifty-five-year-old man who trusted God so completely that he wrote out a list of qualities he wanted in a wife. I had never thought of being that specific.

My prayers changed. I asked God for a wife who loved God and lived according to His word, who would love me and stay by my side. Then I thanked Him for the wife He was going to send. I began telling, my friends: "God is going to send me a wife."

Six months later, I was introduced to a single lady named Joan. She hardly said a word all evening, but I decided to invite her to church. Afterward, Joan invited me to lunch. This time, she had plenty to say and I was impressed: She really was interesting, and she knew her Bible.

Eighteen days later, we were engaged.

People tried to dissuade us. So I went home and got down on my knees and asked the Lord, is Joan the woman You sent? Right away, I knew. Joan loved the Lord and lived according to the Bible, and I would take care of her. I called my seventy-eight-year-old mother to find out what she thought.

"Gill," Mom said, "If you believe God said okay, then go ahead."

Four months after Joan and I met on that August day, and ten months after I'd asked God for a wife who had certain qualities, we were married. This past March, we celebrated our fifth wedding anniversary. These have been happy years, all because I got specific in my prayers, and trusted God.

My Possible Dream

Fran Roberts

A dozen years ago my children and I were in a sorry state. My husband was gone and my health was failing. The doctor said my poor health was caused by the emotional stress of my broken marriage and the physical stress of working two jobs, taking care of our little apartment and trying to be both mother and father to a nine-year-old daughter and an eight-year-old son.

It hadn't always been that way. Only a few years before, we had been a family of four. My husband worked as a milkman and I was a full-time wife and mother, tending not only two young children and our six-room house, but also the chickens, ducks, sheep and pigs we kept on our place in the country—it wasn't really big enough to be called a farm.

It was a life we all enjoyed, but despite counseling, my husband and I grew further and further apart. Eventually we separated, then got a divorce.

The house was sold, and the children and I moved into a three-room apartment. I got a job with a small weekly newspaper for sixty dollars a week.

After about a year, my ex-husband's child support payments became more and more infrequent, and I had to take a second job. To cut expenses, we moved to a cheaper apartment on the edge of a "rough neighborhood" in a nearby city. Soon I was struck down by illness.

The doctor said I would be out of work for some months. With a little money I had set aside from the sale of our house, we were able to get by—barely.

After a couple of months of city apartment living in a depressing neighborhood, every bone in my body cried out for a home of my own with just a little backyard for the children. And one Sunday afternoon I told my friend Lucy about my desire to have my own house.

"You have to face facts," she said, shaking her head sadly. "You're a single woman. You have two small children. You're not getting child support. You're unemployed. You don't have any money.

"I hate to say it, but you don't have a prayer of buying a house."

All that afternoon I thought about her words and I became more and more depressed. Washing the dishes after supper, I turned on the radio for some music, but what I got was the enthusiastic voice of a minister.

"With God, all things are possible," the preacher said, "But you need to know what you want." I took my hand out of the soapsuds. He had my attention now!

"There's nothing wrong with having big dreams," he continued. "After all, the Bible says that if you want to move a mountain, you have to *believe* and say 'be gone from here,' and lo, the mountain will be removed and cast into the sea.

"Start by setting goals—but not fuzzy goals. You can't just say, 'I want a nice house' or 'I want a different job.' You must be specific. Picture in your mind what you want. And *believe* every day."

How extraordinary! It was as though God Almighty was telling me that I did have a prayer, after all.

I turned off the radio and replayed the sermon in my mind. After the children were in bed, I took a notebook and pen and sat down at the kitchen table to begin picturing my house.

What did I want? Well, I wanted a house with a backyard.

"Be specific," the radio voice had said.

"Okay," I said aloud, "I want a two-story house, an older home, with at least three bedrooms, living room, dining room, kitchen and bath. And I'd like to have a porch and an attic and a cellar and a big backyard with an apple tree."

The picture was becoming more clear in my mind.

"I want a maple tree in the front yard and a walk that goes right to the porch; no steps. I'd like a farmhouse-type home with a porch that goes from the front to the side like the letter 'L.' And at the end of the side porch should be a door to the kitchen.

"The kitchen sink should look out over the backyard, and the yard should have enough room for a garden as well as room for the children to play. And I'd like it to be in a quiet neighborhood."

With that, I turned the whole project over to God. I asked His help in achieving my dream and prayed for His blessing upon it. And when I was finished, I felt peaceful and secure, almost as though I had received assurance that I would see my dream come true.

A few months later the doctor said I was able to return to work. I got a job as an associate editor with a business publications firm in New York City. Every day on the train going back and forth from my apartment in New Jersey, I pictured the house and the yard. But as month after month went by, the train's wheels seemed to clack out the message: "No money...no house...no money...no house."

Was my friend right? Was my dream unrealistic?

But then I remembered the radio preacher, and the train

wheels clicked another refrain: "Gotta believe...gotta believe...gotta believe."

After more than a year at the New York City job, I heard of an opening on a small newspaper in a little town in northwestern New Jersey. I rushed over, was interviewed by the editor, was offered a job and accepted on the spot!

The week after I began work there, on my lunch hour, I started calling real estate agents. As soon as they discovered I was divorced, they either found some excuse to get off the telephone or they just told me that there was no point in talking because I'd never get a mortgage.

I was getting more and more discouraged. Was I crazy to have thought it might all work out?

But the very next day I talked with a real estate man who had a different attitude. He said he didn't know why I shouldn't get a mortgage if my income was adequate. Then he asked me to describe the kind of house I was looking for.

When I finished the description, he said, "I'm going out this afternoon to look at a house that sounds a bit like that. Would you like to go with me?"

"I certainly would," I replied.

Late that afternoon we drove down a street less than a mile from the newspaper office. We stopped in front of a house that had an L-shaped porch, a walk leading directly onto that porch (no steps), and a big maple tree in the corner of the property. The street was quiet, too. To the left of the house and all across the street were older homes that the agent said were inhabited by middle-aged and older people. To the right of the house was the town cemetery!

I like Your sense of humor, Lord, I thought as I went up the walk.

The house contained eight rooms: four bedrooms, living room, dining room, kitchen and study. The kitchen sink looked out over the backyard; the backyard contained two apple trees and plenty of room for play and garden areas. And the price was only $15,000.

"Draw up the papers," I said. "This is *my* house."

As I drove home that night, I thanked God for all His blessings.

"Wow, Lord," I said, "You took care of the employment situation and You sent me to the exact house I pictured. Now all I need is money for a down payment."

When I got home I phoned my father and told him about the wonderful house. Then he had some news of his own:

"Remember how the government was negotiating to buy my cabin on the river so they could build that dam?" he asked. "Well, the check arrived this week and I want to give you $1,000 for a down payment and $1,000 for closing costs."

I cried for joy; I was on top of the world. It had taken time and persistence, but my dreams were finally coming true.

I called the real estate agent a few weeks later and asked him how things were progressing.

"The mortgage application is being held up by the FHA," he said. "They haven't turned it down, but they haven't approved it either. It doesn't look good."

I called the president of the mortgage company.

"I personally checked your application, Mrs. Roberts," he said. "Your credit is good, your character is good. As far as I am concerned, you could have the mortgage tomorrow. But it's an FHA loan, and if they don't approve the application, that's the end of it."

"What's the trouble?" I asked.

"You're a divorced woman with two small children," he said bluntly. "The FHA doesn't like to insure money for divorced women. In fact, the FHA doesn't like to insure money for any women.

"You want to know what's ironic?" he asked. "If you were a man with a wife and three small children and another on the way, and you were making the same salary you are making now, they would approve a mortgage for you up to almost $20,000. But because you're a divorced woman, they won't even go for $14,000."

I thanked the man and hung up. I was down, but I wasn't out. I took a deep breath and called the regional office of the FHA. The secretary told me the director was out of town; his assistant was in a meeting. I left my name and number.

Every day for a week I called. Same story. Same message. Same lack of reply.

"Oh, God, I need more help," I cried out one night as I was driving home.

The preacher's voice on the radio came into my mind: "The Bible says that if you want to move a mountain, you have to believe and say, 'be gone from here' and lo, the mountain will be removed and cast into the sea."

As I drove, I pictured a group of frowning men shaking their heads over my mortgage application. I saw them massed into the shape of a mountain. "Be gone from here," I commanded aloud. And then I pictured the mountain sliding off into the sea.

You can do it, Lord, I thought. *I believe in You.*

The next day my editor sent me to a luncheon honoring a member of a major political party. While there, I met several women from the party's state and national headquarters. We got to talking about women's rights—a subject just starting to get nationwide attention.

"I have a special, personal reason for wanting equal rights for women," I said. "I'm trying to buy a house in this town. I earn almost $8,000 a year. I made a deposit of $1,000 on the house and I have $1,000 toward closing costs in the bank. All I need is a $14,000 mortgage, and the FHA won't approve it. The president of the mortgage company told me that the only reason I don't stand a chance of getting the mortgage is because I am a divorced woman."

The others in the group were indignant. "That's the most ridiculous thing I ever heard of," one of them snapped. She took out a business card, and on the back wrote the name and telephone number of a U.S. congressman.

"You tell this man I told you to call," she said. "If anybody can get this thing moving, he's the one. He's a real mountain mover."

A real mountain mover. I felt goose bumps rising on my arms.

When I called the congressman, he promised to look into the matter. "Don't lose hope," he said.

A day after our conversation, I received a photocopy of a letter from the congressman to the FHA office asking for a report on the status of my application.

Two long weeks passed without any further word. Then one night I came home exhausted. I leafed through the mail—a bill...a pamphlet...and an envelope from the congressman's office! I tore it open and skimmed the words in a copy of a letter he had received from the FHA: "...you will be interested to know that a determination has been made...and the mortgage application has been approved."

Now my eyes were so full of tears I couldn't read any farther.

I've been in my house eleven years now. The children have grown up and have gone out on their own. Just as I do, they carry the knowledge that with God all things *are* possible. Because in the years before equal loans for women were guaranteed by law, their mother was able to buy the dream house she envisioned and God provided.

In Our Tender Care

Lynn Thurman

I gazed at the white-gowned angel at the top of our Christmas tree. "Next year," I thought aloud, "We'll have another angel with us."

Jerry wrapped his arms around me. "Just two more weeks until the baby is here," he said.

After three miscarriages in eleven years, I'd been told by our doctor, "No more," I could not have children. Then a co-worker informed me that one of his friends was three months pregnant, out of work and a single parent already caring for two children. She was considering giving the baby up for adoption. He put us in touch with the woman, and we talked on the telephone.

She agreed to let us adopt the baby. Our first meeting came a few days later, and we made all the legal arrangements.

During the next six months I went with the woman on her regular trips to the doctor. I'll never forget the first visit, when she introduced me as the baby's mother. As the delivery date approached, I excitedly filled the baby's room with teddy bears and clothing. Beneath our tree I even had gifts to give the woman's two children, a small gesture considering the gift she was going to give me.

On the day before Christmas, word came that she was in labor. I didn't make it in time for the delivery, but as soon as I entered her hospital room, my benefactor said, "It's a girl. Merry Christmas, Mom."

I wasn't permitted to see the baby right away. Jerry, my friend, Arlene and I went with the birth mother's sister to the waiting room. Then the doctor came in, pulled a table over and sat on the edge of it. He looked me squarely in the eye. "Are you prepared," he said, "to raise a baby who is biracial?"

It took a few minutes for his shocking words to sink in, not because I feel any prejudice, but because a newborn's happiness was at stake. What would be the right decision for *her*? I rushed to the mother's room. "Why didn't you tell me this?" I cried.

"I was afraid you would back out," she said. "You don't have to go through with the adoption. I'll keep the baby."

"I need time to think," I answered.

On the way home Jerry and Arlene tried to console me, but all I could do was cry. The Christmas lights along the road passed in a blur of confusion.

The house seemed bleak as we entered it. Jerry immediately went to the phone and called our minister, who came and spent several hours talking with us and listening.

"Lynn," he asked, "What did we all pray for?"

"A healthy baby girl," I replied.

"And what did God give you?" he asked.

"A healthy baby girl," I said.

Jerry made his decision at that moment: We had received the blessing we had prayed for, and he wanted the baby. So did I, but I still needed reassurance that we were up to the challenge. I feared the pitfalls that might come from her being raised in a white environment. Would she be denied her heritage in the black community? I wanted the best for the baby, and I was willing to give her up if that was the best thing to do.

Late Christmas Eve the mother called to say she had signed

the papers that allowed Jerry and me to visit the hospital nursery and feed the baby. The mother was going home, but would get in touch with us after Christmas for our decision.

On Christmas morning my heart was heavy as we prepared to go to my parents' house for breakfast. I hadn't let them know about the baby's birth; I wanted to be sure of my decision before I told anyone. I'd been raised by a prejudiced dad, and I feared his reaction.

We excused ourselves as soon as we could and went to the hospital. For the first time I took the baby in my arms, while Jerry went to get a bottle of formula. I found a rocker, sat down and studied the small sleeping form. An elderly black man stood nearby, gazing at an infant in an incubator. "May I talk with you a minute?" I asked.

"Yes," he said, and explained that the baby in the incubator was his granddaughter. He bent down and looked at the bundle I cradled.

"Do you think I can do this child justice if I adopt her?" I asked.

He placed his hand on my shoulder and said, "All you have to do is love her."

I looked at the baby, who seemed so secure in my arms, and I started to rock her and sing to her. I remembered Jesus' words to his disciples after he had calmed the sea: "You of little faith, why are you so afraid?"

This Christmas Eve Molly will be two years old. Yes, there have been a few incidents of racism shown to us, but so far we have been able to handle them, and I know that with the Lord's help, we will continue to do so. Molly is a joy to everyone, including my dad. Just as God planned the birth of our Savior nearly two thousand years ago, I am sure he also planned the birth of Molly on Christmas Eve and gave her to us to love.

The Best Christmas Gift

Marion Lott

My father was in the Phelps Memorial Hospital in North Tarrytown, recovering from surgery. He had his leg amputated above his knee due to poor circulation and was very depressed since he was not going to be able to spend his granddaughter's first Christmas with her.

My husband and I were in the process of building a house and we were living with my parents, along with our eight-month-old daughter, Amanda. She was grandpa's pride and joy.

Now a little history: My outgoing father had worked at Guideposts for about six years, in what used to be called the Print Shop. He enjoyed working with all the guys who were much younger than he was, but he was especially fond of his supervisor, Earl. Earl was also a member of a local volunteer ambulance group as was Herman, one of the vendors who came into Guideposts quite often. Both Earl and Herman knew that my father was in the hospital and would not be able to get home Christmas day.

It was about 6:00 A.M. Christmas morning. My mother had been awake for about thirty minutes and I had just gotten up to dress and feed our daughter. All of a sudden, there was a loud knock at the back door of the house. My mom went to answer the door and when she opened it she let out a loud cry of joy and happiness. Earl and Herman were standing on the back door landing. Herman was carrying a folded wheelchair and Earl was carrying my father! In the driveway was an ambulance.

I came out to see what the noise and excitement was about and there was my father, sitting in his wheelchair, smiling from ear to ear, holding his granddaughter on his lap. Tears came to my eyes and I went over to both Earl and Herman and gave them hugs and kisses. I asked them how they managed this, how were they able to get my father out of the hospital? How were they able to leave their families Christmas morning? Why did they do this?

The only answer they would give was that they wanted my father to be with his family and his granddaughter...to see her open her toys.

Around 8:00 P.M., Earl and Herman came back to the house and drove my dad back to the hospital.

To this day we have no idea how Earl and Herman managed to sign my father out and get him home for Christmas. You know what. It doesn't matter. I will always remember that Christmas. Earl and Herman's loving, caring friendship was the best gift my family and I could ever or would ever receive.

Trust God for Everything

Millie Tharle

Two years ago my husband, age forty-seven, died very suddenly of a massive heart attack. We had one daughter, age nineteen, home from college for the summer when he died.

After the funeral and after the friends went back to their daily lives, I was in such a sad state, but hid it well to assure my daughter that I would be fine, and she could go back to college away from home. I did not know how, but I knew I would be.

Several things happened that made me know God was looking out for us. First, my job sent me away from home during the week traveling with old friends so I was rarely home alone. Weekends my daughter came home to be with me. Then I prayed about our house. It was big with lots of yard to keep. I did not know how long I could handle it and the additional expenses without a second income. Plus, my job was thirty-two miles from home.

I put the house up for sale in less than a year and nothing happened. I was unhappy that no one seemed interested, but after six months, I resigned myself to staying put.

During that time, I learned I could live alone. I could keep the house and yard and I could make ends meet, as long as I put my trust in God for everything.

After about eighteen months passed I felt I should try to sell the house again and I prayed for God to tell me where he wanted us to move. My daughter decided to come home that summer and live with me and go to school locally. My house sold in about two months for the asking price, and I found a wonderful condo close to my daughter's school and my work place. The timing was perfect, but then, everything God does is that way. He answers His way and in His time.

Goodbye and Hello

Margaret Bosley

I wanted to attend my grandmother's funeral. I was too young to be at my other grandparents' funerals. The airline flights cost too much and I did not trust myself to drive alone in the car for eight hours.

I found no other solution except to take some time off from work and go to my church at the time of her funeral to privately celebrate my grandmother with God.

I e-mailed my oldest sister and told her that I would not be able to attend the funeral. My heart was heavy. I said a quick prayer giving God my problem. If He wanted me to be at the funeral, He would have to get me there.

I no sooner sent the message when my stepmother called. My father died eight years ago and I hadn't talked to my stepmother in a couple of years. My grandmother was still her mother-in-law, and she said she needed closure to her death. She invited me to ride with her up to New York for the funeral. Tears streamed down my face as I told her, "Yes."

We stayed at one of my older sister's houses. When I got to the viewing, I talked with my cousins about old times and memories of my grandmother. We looked at pictures of my grandmother on her wedding day and when she was young. What a treat to see her then.

I turned around and saw someone come in that looked like my youngest brother. I did a double take. It *was* my youngest brother. He unexpectedly got a flight and decided to come and be with grandmother one last time. I gave him a big hug and thanked the Lord for getting me there to say one last goodbye to my grandmother and one more precious hello to my baby brother.

Proven Faithful

Jeannie Scott

A few years ago, I went to work for a state politician as an administrative assistant, appointed to handle constituent correspondence. For a single young woman, the salary was just the right amount to live comfortably and put some in savings as well. In fact, after about a year and a half, I built a garden home in a new neighborhood. My life couldn't have been any better.

Then, one week before Christmas, my supervisor fired me to hire her sister. I was very upset. I had just closed on my house the week before and now I was unemployed. I hated my employer for waiting until Christmas, and I was mad at God for allowing this to happen to me. Why did He let me buy the house, just to lose it? I had enough savings to last for awhile, but I was afraid. Every night I prayed that God would provide, but I had my doubts that I would be able to keep my house.

After a couple of months, I mentioned to my friend, Charlotte, that I would sell my house if God didn't provide a job for me in the next two weeks. She replied, "Why are you dictating your terms to God? He isn't telling you to sell your house. You are afraid and aren't trusting Him. Keep the house and trust that He will provide. You never know what God will do."

Sure enough, after another month, I received a job offer from a nonprofit agency to head up their grassroots volunteers. Best of all, the salary was significantly more than I had been making. If I had stuck to my original plan to sell the house, I might have missed out on the blessings God had in store for me. I don't understand why God works the way He does, but he proved faithful, just as He promised. He turned a bad situation into joy, and strengthened my faith in the process.

The Miracle House

Rosalie Morrow

For seventeen years I prayed specifically for my own house; three bedrooms on one floor, with central air conditioning, Berber carpeting and close to my church.

One September, we were living in a small duplex (less than five hundred square feet) when a large house came up for sale down the street. A friend and I passed the house one day and she remarked to me that I should try to buy that house. I called a real estate agent from my church and began to seek information. When I spoke to the real estate agent, I asked her to see if the owner would sell on contract or "rent-to-own" because I was sure we would not be able to secure a mortgage because of past credit problems. She told me that we should try for the mortgage first.

A few days later, the agent put me in touch with a mortgage broker and within twenty-four hours we were prequalified. Within two weeks of finding the house and being preapproved for the mortgage, my father-in-law's estate was settled and my husband received his inheritance.

We made an offer on the house. The owners came back with a slightly higher counter offer, and we accepted it. The owners had painted the house inside and were having a new roof put on the house during negotiations.

With the estate money in our hands, we decided to put $4,000 down on the house. The week before closing, the real estate agent (who had become a trusted friend) called and said we would only need to put $2,500 down on the house. The next day that amount dropped to $2,000. The next day it dropped to $1,500. The day of closing, she called and said, "All you need to put down is $1,298!" So, with the extra money, we were able to purchase the new appliances we needed.

We signed the closing papers on the sale of the house and moved in three days later.

Living in this house is still a miracle to me. God does answer prayer. Sometimes it just takes a little while.

My New Job

Harriet Smith

Several years ago, I sent a prayer request to Guideposts for direction. My job had been eliminated by downsizing, and my unemployment had run out. We'd moved to a smaller house and still no job.

Well, God had a marvelous plan for me when I finally took time to listen and trust Him completely.

My daughter attends a Christian school and even through those tough times, we made sure she remained there. I was involved with her class trips and projects, but that was not all.

One Sunday there was an employment opportunity listed in our church bulletin for a secretarial position at the school. I was quickened to apply for the job, even though it was just part-time. It really wasn't what I was looking for, but that's what I found.

So I started working at the school. That was five years ago. I'm now a full-time teacher's assistant (for four years now) and love every second of it! God knew that would be my ministry but had to get my attention to get me to know it.

I don't make near the money I used to make but God is sufficient...all of our bills are being paid thanks to God's provisions.

Thank you for your continued prayers and praise to God for His Mysterious Ways!

Prayer Works

David Hagberg

As a young person, I had my first drink of a beverage containing alcohol and I loved what it did for me. Fifteen years later, I had my last drink of alcohol. In the years in between, havoc and fear gripped me, friends and my first wife left me, and much wreckage was in my wake.

During the early morning hours of a December day, I got down on my knees and prayed two words: "God, help!" Since that day, I have not even had a desire to drink nor a craving for alcohol. My life has straightened out. I have a wonderful wife, a good job and many fantastic friends. There is a lot more to the story, but I wanted to keep it simple. Yes, God interceded in my life because of my simple prayer. Prayer works!

The Wallet

Shirley Forsyth

One Sunday afternoon I was going out with my husband and son to shop and return a videotape. As we left the house I was carrying my husband's wallet, the videotape and several other items in an awkward bundle.

My husband went into the store to return the video while Connor and I stayed in the car. When he came back, he asked if I had his wallet. I said it was in the back seat. After looking I saw that it wasn't there. Needless to say, he was not amused.

We drove home and looked in the driveway, on the porch, and throughout the house in minute detail to no avail. By this point my husband was quite enraged. We began to make a list of what was in the wallet—credit cards, health card, driver's license, ownership and registration, video store membership card, along with things we couldn't replace, like pictures of Connor. Luckily Michael does not keep money in his wallet. We phoned the credit card companies and video store and cancelled the accounts. My husband began to bemoan the amount of time he would have to spend to replace all his identification.

Throughout this fiasco I kept saying a little prayer: "Please, Lord, let us find the wallet or have the person who found it return it to us." As the evening wore on, whenever the phone rang, I hoped that it would be someone reporting that the wallet was found.

Monday morning, I got up early and went to work. Midway through the morning Michael called. He had gone out to get the morning paper and noticed a little package, the size of a sample bar of soap, on the porch steps. When he got closer, he realized it was not soap. It was the entire contents of his wallet. All of his credit cards and identification along with photos and receipts.

Michael was amazed at this. He said, "Who would keep the wallet and return the contents? After all, the wallet itself isn't important."

I knew the answer. Thank You, Lord, for answering my prayer.

Bette Davis and Me

Mary Wheatley Van Hoosan

I stood there amazed as I saw the man tumble down the spiral staircase of the old southern mansion and sprawl on the hall floor. Stony-faced and triumphant, a petite woman looked down on him from the top of the stairs. There was silence, and then someone shouted, "Cut!" The director snapped, "It's a wrap."

People on the set moved. The "husband" was helped up. And the woman smiled, walked down the stairs and turned toward the soundstage exit. I couldn't believe my luck. Bette Davis was only five feet away!

I was a starry-eyed college student from a small Oklahoma town, on vacation in Hollywood, where I had managed to wrangle a job as a cub reporter for the *Citizen News*. If I landed an interview with a star, I would receive a bonus of fifteen dollars. But I had even greater plans. As God knew from my endless prayers, I wanted someday to be a star myself.

I'd learned from reading *Daily Variety* which movies were being shot that day. A friend who owned a sandwich truck hid me under a tarpaulin when he went to one of the studios. The guard waved us through and I was let out in a remote back lot.

"Don't let anyone know how you got in," my friend whispered. "You'll need a pass to get out."

I'd wandered down the back alleys of the studio, pinching myself because I felt so lucky. Suddenly I noticed a soundstage door that was ajar, and soon found myself in a maze of boxes and coiling cables. Almost instantly the door closed and a red light began to flash. "Quiet on the set," someone shouted. I had stumbled upon the filming of a scene from *The Little Foxes.*

As I watched the actors work I thought, *I'm in trouble now.* My dream of stardom would probably get me as far as the Hollywood police station.

But when the filming was over and Miss Davis was walking my way, I knew I had to approach her. I'd been told that to get in the movies you should know somebody important. After meeting Bette Davis, I could give up college and soon have my name in lights.

I pulled my notebook and camera from my purse. "Miss Davis," I stammered, "may I interview you?"

She looked me over, those enormous eyes taking me in. "Certainly," she said. "Why don't we go out in the sunlight where you can take a picture?"

After our photography session, we walked to her trailer, where we sat in director-style folding chairs. I was so tongue-tied I could only stare. She had such small hands and tiny feet. She kept brushing away strands of hair. Finally I remembered my notebook and began writing. She talked.

"Getting a break may be the start of an acting career," she said, "but any talent from the Almighty must be honed with rock-gut determination. And this applies to any career where the Almighty leads you."

I scribbled.

"I suppose you want to quit school and become a famous actress yourself?" she asked.

I sheepishly admitted that was my plan.

"Stay in school," she said. "Get a degree so you will have something if the acting doesn't work out."

She rose from her chair. The interview was over. Then she asked the question I was dreading: "How did you get into the studio?"

I had to tell the truth. Her reaction to my frightened explanation was one of the most musical laughs I ever heard.

"Well, my dear, that is some way to crash the gates!" Taking my hand, she led me to the front. "This girl is a member of the press," she announced to the security guard. I was home free.

Back in the offices of the *Citizen News* I delivered my interview and a surprised editor paid me the fifteen dollar bonus. And when the summer was over, I did just as Miss Davis said. I returned to the University of Oklahoma and became a teacher, a career that gave me great satisfaction and pleasure.

Many years later, when Bette Davis was in her seventies, she came to my town to deliver a talk. At the end there was a question-and-answer period. I stood up and told her how we had met forty years before and how she had helped me. Later she sent me a note, glad to have heard the story. I keep it on my wall today, framed. It reminds me that God answers all our prayers, even if his answer is not quite the one we expect.

CHAPTER 6

But this I call to mind,

and therefore I have hope:

The steadfast love of the Lord

never ceases,

his mercies never come to an end;

they are new every morning;

great is your faithfulness.

"The Lord is my portion," says my soul,

"therefore I will hope in him."

LAMENTATIONS 3:21-24 *(NRSV)*

Prayer Changes Those Who Pray

Why do I close my eyes

When I speak to You, Lord?

I used to tell myself that it was because

I wanted no distractions

To concentrate entirely on You.

But now I think it's also because

With my eyes closed, I am a child again,

Vulnerable, defenseless, dependent on You.

When I'm at rest in Your arms,

There is only one security:

You.

RICK HAMLIN

In Spite of Spite

Carol A. Virgil

I knew something was wrong as soon as my thirteen-year-old daughter, Teresa, walked in.

"I'm really mad this time," she began, biting her bottom lip to keep it from quivering. She tossed a book in my lap and sank down into a chair across the room.

I recognized the book as one she had just bought. She loves to read and is always buying new books. I held it up and looked at her quizzically.

"Look inside the back cover," was all she said before she turned to gaze out of the window.

I flipped open the back over and saw: "I hate you, you're ugly and you're scum." The hastily written words were barely legible, small and pinched looking, but the impact was the same as if they had been on a billboard along the freeway.

"Did Brooke do this?" I asked as Teresa turned from the window.

She nodded, spilling a single tear over a brimming eyelid. Instantly my motherly instincts kicked in. What kind of hateful, spiteful child would do such a thing?

Ever since we'd moved to Oregon, this girl had been a thorn in Teresa's side. Teresa had been able—until now—to ignore her.

That's what we'd taught our three girls to do. "If kids start picking on you," we'd always say, "don't stoop to their level. Instead,
just ignore them. They'll get tired of it when they see they aren't
getting any response."

Right now, however, I wanted to do anything but ignore this
child. I wanted to punch her lights out. There was no excuse for
her cruel behavior.

"Mom..." Teresa's weak voice made me take my eyes off
those awful words. "I just don't know what I could have done to
make her hate me so much."

"Oh, Teresa, you simply showed up. For some people, that's
all it takes. You're a good kid and I'm proud of the way you've
handled yourself these last few weeks. I know it hasn't been easy
for you."

It hadn't either—for any of us, but for the girls especially.
We'd just been through a cross-country move, from the plains of
Minnesota to the Willamette Valley of Oregon. Teresa left a class
of twenty-seven eighth-graders she'd grown up with and was
thrust into a class of over two hundred. For someone as quiet
and shy as Teresa, it had been overwhelming. The last thing she
needed was some balloon-headed adolescent being malicious.

What could I say to help my daughter? She was at that age
when what your peers think of you matters so much. How could
I help her cope? Had our advice been wrong? Should we have
taught our children to be more aggressive?

"You know what you should say to her tomorrow?" I heard
myself contemplating out loud. "You should say, 'You think I'm
ugly? Have you looked in a mirror lately?'"

This brought a surprised smirk to Teresa's face, and as her sisters began to drift home from school, we all got into the act of
thinking up different witty things to say to put Brooke in her
place. Of course, we all knew that Teresa was too tenderhearted

to say any of them, but we got Teresa smiling, and at least she knew the home front was on her side.

Each day I began asking Teresa for a "Brooke Report." What happened today? What did she do? What did you do? I began to notice that both of us were developing an unhealthy attitude about the girl. Every time I thought of those terrible words written in the back of Teresa's book, I'd get mad all over again. I knew deep in my heart that I was not handling this situation in an adult manner, let alone godly, but I didn't care. Brooke was wrong to treat anybody that way, especially my daughter!

About a week later, when I wasn't even thinking about "that girl," I stumbled across my old kindergarten diploma while rummaging through some boxes. Moving has a way of unearthing relics. I hadn't seen the thing in years. I picked it up and fondly ran my finger along its soft royal blue cover.

I distinctly remembered two things about kindergarten—Mrs. Lidke, our much-loved teacher, and Rebecca. I hadn't thought about them in years.

Scenes came rushing back to me as if someone had slipped a movie into a videocassette recorder. My class was standing behind a divider that separated the coat area from the classroom. Rebecca, a homely, slow student, was an easy target for ridicule. I, a fiery redhead, was being egged on by some of the other girls.

"I hate you!" I was saying through gritted teeth to Rebecca. I was enjoying Rebecca's discomfort, but even more, I relished the approval of the other girls. I sharpened my tongue and lashed out again, "I hate you. You're ugly, and you're stupid."

Just then Mrs. Lidke came around the corner of the divider. She had heard the whole thing. Rebecca was in tears by this time. Mrs. Lidke put a comforting hand on her shoulder and, looking right at me, said, "Carol, I'm surprised. I expected so much more from you."

As if in a freeze-frame, I could still see genuine surprise and outright disappointment in Mrs. Lidke's eyes. I had been a bully. I was—what had I called Brooke—a mean, spiteful, hateful child?

At first I tried to rationalize a difference between the two situations. After all, I had been only six. But no matter how hard I tried to pretend it wasn't the same thing, those words kept coming back to me: "Carol, I expected so much more from you."

I remember the shame I felt that day; even at that tender age I knew it wasn't right to hurt someone. I told Rebecca I was sorry. Afterward I always tried to be nice to her, even when other kids were being mean.

Now, all these years later, I began to wonder. Why had I taunted Rebecca? Certainly it was nothing Rebecca had ever done; she was just there, frightened and shy. But so was I. I was frightened that the other girls wouldn't like me, and I used Rebecca to prove I was strong. I think I had known it all along. Brooke wasn't really mean and spiteful. She was an insecure girl trying to gain her peers' approval. And Teresa happened to be an easy target because she was new and quiet.

Now I knew that God, just like Mrs. Lidke, expected more of me than daily "Brooke Reports" and spite-filled chatter. In truth, I expected more of myself. I searched my Bible and found in Colossians what I already knew to be right. "Therefore, as God's chosen people, holy and dearly loved, clothe yourself with compassion, kindness, humility, gentleness and patience. Bear with each other and forgive whatever grievances you may have against one another. Forgive as the Lord forgave you." (3:12,13, *NIV*).

I carefully wrote out the verses, and laid the note on Teresa's bed where she'd be sure to see it. Later, after she got home, I went to her room and told her my story about the little redheaded girl in my kindergarten class and explained how she really just wanted to be accepted.

"I think I was luckier than Brooke," I explained to her. "I had someone who had truly believed I was above that sort of thing. And knowing that Mrs. Lidke thought I was better made me *want* to be better. Maybe Brooke does these things because she doesn't know just how special she is to God."

Teresa gave me a look that said: *Brooke? Special?* But she conceded, "I never thought of it that way before. I guess I can try to be nice to her."

So together we prayed for Brooke and for God's help in forgiving her. As yet, Brooke has not changed. But Teresa and I have. By clothing ourselves in feelings of compassion and kindness, we have rid ourselves of resentment and spite.

One day before the school year was out, Teresa came home with a big grin and handed me a note. It was from one of the girls Brooke had befriended. She wrote that she felt "really bad about Brooke's bad attitude" toward Teresa and that she "really admired" the way Teresa was handling it.

So, thank you, Mrs. Lidke, for bringing back Teresa's smile...and for showing a grateful mother and daughter that spite is never a match for kindness.

A Reason to Be Thankful

Louis A. Hill

When my doctor detected a slight irregularity in my prostate gland during an annual checkup three and a half years ago, I asked my wife, Jeanne, to join me in prayer that it would not be cancer. Then we waited anxiously for the results of my PSA (prostate-specific antigen) test, which can detect prostate malignancies.

My doctor called with news of an abnormal PSA level. A biopsy confirmed cancer. Jeanne made two phone calls for me: one to cancel our fortieth anniversary cruise, which we'd been planning for years, and the other to schedule surgery at Barnes Hospital at Washington University Medical Center in St. Louis.

I was shaken. I had always passed my yearly physicals. Jeanne and I exercised and lived healthily. Before leaving Arizona for Barnes Hospital, I asked the members of my Sunday school to pray. "If cancer has reached my lymph nodes," I said, "I'll stand just a fifteen percent chance of recovery. Please pray that cancer isn't in those nodes and that my surgery is successful." We prayed right then, and I felt comforted when they assured me of their continued prayers.

On the day my wife and I were to have set sail on our cruise, we flew to St. Louis instead, and rented an apartment near the hospital. At 6:00 A.M. the next day I went into surgery.

When I regained consciousness, the afternoon sun was too low; I knew something had gone wrong. "What happened?" I asked Jeanne.

"Cancer was *not* in your lymph nodes," she quickly assured me, "but it had spread beyond your prostate. Dr. Catalona cut as wide a swath as possible around it. Though we can't be sure until the lab report, the doctor hopes he got it all. You need rest. Just concentrate on getting well."

I tried my best to be a good patient. Walking was part of the recovery plan, so when I was released five days later, I took long walks around the apartment complex. I went with Jeanne through the parking lot into a wooded area, where she spotted a brown, velvety bunny that brightened her spirits. But waiting for that lab report weighed heavily on me.

When Dr. Catalona summoned Jeanne and me to his office, I feared bad news. "The lab report," he said, "shows microscopic extension of the cancer to the edge of your prostate gland in two places." He drew a diagram of the locations. "That means to be absolutely safe you should have radiation on those spots after your surgery heals."

I froze with fear, remembering a similar diagram in an article I'd read. "Aren't those the spots where radiation could damage my colon so badly that it might not function?" I asked. The doctor nodded.

But he warned, "If you don't have the radiation now, you must get a PSA test at least every six months—or every three months if you want to be careful—for the rest of your life. If your PSA goes above zero-point-six, you must have radiation." My heart sank. I'd be waiting the rest of my life for that other shoe to drop.

"I feel as if a silent killer were stalking me!" I blurted out. "How could I have so much cancer without any symptoms and without it showing up on my annual exam?

Dr. Catalona looked weary. "Louis, I just wish I could get word out to every man over fifty to have a PSA test yearly to help catch prostate cancer before it spreads." He scheduled me for a PSA test that day.

"The next morning he telephoned. "Your test showed zero-point-seven. It's quite soon after surgery, so it could be off," he said. "But if it's still this high when your surgery is healed, you must have radiation."

I didn't sleep that night, or the next. Just before dawn I asked myself, *What kind of life am I going to have, holding my breath from one test to the next? Lord, it doesn't seem fair.*

When Jeanne got up to fix breakfast, I tried to act rested, not wanting to drag her into my pit of fear and doubt. After breakfast Jeanne said gently, "Louis, it's time for your walk. The fresh air will—"

"I don't feel like a walk!" I raged.

After lunch Jeanne took the bus to Barnes on the pretext of looking into insurance payments. She returned with an armload of books about living positively with cancer.

"I don't want to read them," I snapped. "They're just a bunch of Pollyanna hooey!" Jeanne bit her lip. I knew she was hurt, but I couldn't comfort her. I was hurting too.

At bedtime Jeanne rubbed my back, trying to help me get to sleep. It didn't work, but I pretended to nod off so she could stop and get some rest herself. Soon I heard her even breathing. Hours later, I finally dozed.

Suddenly I woke up. Someone was shaking my shoulder. I lay there a moment, trying to get my wits about me. My shoulder was shaken again.

"Yes? What is it?" I whispered.

Jeanne didn't answer.

Annoyed, I turned over and asked her, "What do you want?"

But Jeanne was sound asleep.

Who had shaken me?

Suddenly I knew who. I sat bolt upright in bed. Unmistakably, I felt a presence in the room. My heart hammered. I whispered, "Yes, Lord?"

I felt his words, rather than heard them. But the message was distinct. *You haven't thanked me! Remember the lepers?* I sat there awestruck. Then I felt his presence fade.

I sucked in my breath. I'd been feeling so sorry for myself that I had forgotten. God *had* answered my prayer that cancer would not be in my lymph nodes. It wasn't. But, like nine of the ten lepers the Lord healed, I had not thanked him. "Give thanks in all circumstances" (I Thessalonians 5:18) the Bible says. I was ashamed.

Right then I scrambled out of bed and knelt. *Lord, I've been so afraid. Please forgive me for not acknowledging your answer. But I am thankful. Help me get over my fear and to live confidently.* I climbed back into bed and was asleep within minutes.

The next morning when Jeanne woke up she found me propped up in bed reading. "I was wrong about the books," I told her sheepishly, "and this one's already given me some good tips." Jeanne beamed. Then I told her about my visitor.

Right after breakfast I set out on a walk. As soon as I got to the wooded area, Jeanne's bunny hopped in front of my path and wrinkled its nose. A wave of thankfulness washed over me. "Oh, Lord," I said aloud, "thanks for sending along Jeanne's bunny and for the cheerful people I just spoke to in the parking lot. Thank you that the flowers are in bloom. And thank you most of all for Jeanne—for loving me when I've been unlovable."

On our flight home to Arizona I asked Jeanne if she would help me make a "Thanks supper" for all the people who had prayed for me.

"Louis," she said, hugging me, "I'll not only help you, but I'll bake us a great big cake!"

That cake took up nearly half our dining room table, had bold red lettering that declared, "Thanks to God and to Those Who Prayed," and, along with a delicious ham supper, easily fed my forty-five prayer partners.

A month later I called for the results of my most recent PSA test. I had prepared myself for the eventuality of radiation treatments. But I was not prepared for the lab technician's news. "You tested at zero-point-four," he said. I was fine.

Ever since then my PSA tests have all been clean. Jeanne and I continue to visit frequently with God in prayer. And I remain forever grateful to him for restoring the thankfulness in my heart.

Trust in Me

Jennifer Schroeder

For years I had been waging a battle with my own fear. I was like "Chicken Little" running around afraid the sky was falling. I spent sleepless nights worrying about what might happen if: my husband lost his job; the car broke down; my children got sick.

My mother used to tell me that I feared because I lacked faith. I knew to some extent she was right. However, I couldn't get around the feeling that if I stopped worrying, I wouldn't be prepared if something big happened. If I let down and felt happy, I'd be blindsided by one of life's obstacles.

I learned this defense mechanism as a child. I saw so many good people stricken with illness, tragedy, and strife. Where was God in their case? I believed God didn't interfere with everyday issues. God let us have our free will and the experience of the consequences that came with our choices. I was never happy for any length of time. I resented God for abandoning me. He never seemed to answer my prayers. My mother never got better, her pain never went away, and the car always seemed to break down when finances were thinnest. My life was in chaos.

One morning, my neighbor left some donuts with a little note at my doorstep. The note included a passage from the Bible: Jeremiah 29:11, 13 (*NRSV*): *For surely I know the plans I have*

*for you, says the Lord, plans for your welfare and not for harm,
to give you a future with hope.... When you search for me, you
will find me; if you seek me with all your heart.* That day, I reded-
icated my life to Jesus Christ.

In my search for God, I read some Christian literature that
pointed out that often we ask the Lord for "stuff" when we
should be asking for the ability to handle what comes. That really hit home for me. I began praying that God take my fear and
anxiety from me. I said over and over, "I can do all things
through Him who strengthens me." When the fear would creep
in, I'd pray that the Lord help me use the gifts He'd given me to
handle the situation and that He'd help me to be courageous in
the face of my fear. It was difficult, and at first, I didn't do very
well. Then one day, my toddler was hollering at me to get her a
drink. She was fretting that she wouldn't get what she wanted.
Out of my mouth came words that rang in my ears. "If you trust
me, I'll give you what you need." It was like someone took me by
the shoulders and shook me. I immediately wrote that on a piece
of paper and put it on my refrigerator. I looked up at heaven and
said, "O.K., God, I hear ya. I got it!"

About two months later, we hit some really difficult financial
times. Finances had always been a big trigger for my fears.
When my husband told me that I'd have to stretch the diapers
we had for our two children longer than I knew we could, I
prayed. I prayed that the Lord would help me to be clever and
thoughtful. I also prayed that He take my fear from me so that
my thinking would not be clouded. After I was finished, my
heart was light and my mind was full of ideas. I was able to sleep
that night, and I awoke ready to tackle the new day. Later that
day, my husband called the credit union to check on the avail-
ability of some funds in our savings account. He discovered that
a savings account he thought had been closed was, in fact, open

and receiving deposits every pay check. There was a substantial amount of money in that account. It was like God wrote us a check and handed it to us.

I started to cry. I was so grateful. I got on my knees and thanked God. I didn't thank Him just for the money, but for the strength and courage to do what needed to be done when I didn't know what was around the corner. I knew if I trusted Him, He'd give me what I needed.

Two years ago my wife was traveling home to our ranch from church one Sunday with our son and was involved in a terrible car accident. During her last days of life, she made me promise I would raise our son to the absolute best of my ability. My son regained his health and I tried to be the best parent possible. But it just seemed like the harder I tried, the less I saw happening.

My son was not in trouble, but it just seemed that he wasn't able to handle all that had happened in his life. I tried time and time again to help him and encourage him, but to no avail. I was chopping away, but no wood chips were flying.

I have always believed in God and knew that I had to keep praying. I prayed prayers of blessing for my son and then prayed some more. Despite my fervent prayers, his characteristically solid grades in school began to suffer. I considered therapy but decided I couldn't depend on a therapist every time there was a problem in our home.

I kept my eyes and ears open, knowing that God can bring help from an unexpected direction while you are looking elsewhere. That's what happened to me.

One day I was in an office supply store when I spied a discount book rack. I often look at such books but had never seen one in this type of store before. I picked up a little book, opened it, and found it fascinating. I had to have it. I went straight home and began reading that very night. This slim volume contained stories that also contained answers to the problems I was then facing. I rationed out the stories, limiting myself to no more than two stories each evening. Eureka! At last I had found the source of help I needed.

Did I receive the answers to problems that my son was having? Absolutely! I knew the book was heaven sent. After I finished that book, I found others by the same author and kept learning and putting what I read about into practice.

By this time my son and I had achieved major success. Today my son is a different person. I found out my son was harboring feelings of guilt because he was not able to do more for his mom on the day of their car accident. He was living in fear of losing me too.

That book I picked up was *The Promise of Prayer* published by some outfit called Guideposts. God had listened to my prayers, and when I was prepared to listen, I found the life changing answers I needed between the pages of a book while running a simple errand.

Never Alone

Carol Hailey

My car kicked up dust as I wound along the freshly graded dirt road toward the summer camp. The drive from Albuquerque through the Manzano Mountains had taken little more than an hour.

Every summer for the last eight years, my husband and I had brought our two sons here for a week. When Jim and Gary were young, they came as campers. After they reached high school age they worked as counselors. This trip was always our family time.

This was the first time I had come alone.

As I passed the sight that read, "Sandia Summer Camp," I caught my first glimpse of the baseball fields and recreation area. I drove past the recreational vehicles and trailers and parked my car in the gravel parking lot.

With my duffle bag over my shoulder, my make-up kit in one hand, tote bag filled with class material for my Bible class in the other, and a pillow stuffed under my left arm, I made my way carefully down the steep, rocky path to the main camp. Above the trees, I could see the old, iron school bell perched atop its pole. I wondered if it would be there by the end of the week. Every year, some mischievous camper removed it from its pole and hid it from the counselors.

Why would this year be any different? I thought.

The cabins and dormitories were filled with one hundred fifty enthusiastic campers. The sun was shining brightly through the trees, and I knew it would be a fun-filled week. It wasn't right that I felt so alone.

As I rounded the corner of the main building, Charles Burnett, the camp director greeted me. "I hope you won't mind bunking upstairs." He said. "The couples' bedrooms downstairs are all filled. Go right up those stairs and make yourself at home. You may even be the only one up there this session."

I struggled down the narrow hallway, past the couples' bedrooms where I had always stayed in earlier years, and up the steep, wooden stairs to the old dorm room.

In the dim light coming from the single window at the far end of the room, I saw the metal skeletons of twenty army cots and a stack of mattresses.

I lugged my load to the far end and opted for a bed with a view. I dragged my mattress across the floor and made my bed. The old bed squeaked and groaned as I sat in the middle of it. Through the window, I could see the classroom building and two of the new dorms. I caught my breath as I watched the campers scurrying between the buildings.

"Lord," I prayed, "please help me to focus on sharing You and Your word with these young people. Today is Your gift. And, Lord, please help me not to feel so alone. In the name of Jesus, Amen."

Following supper and group singing in the recreation hall, I again climbed to my lonely loft. The bare light bulb in the center of the room gave off just enough light for me to read over my Bible lessons for the week.

I pulled the string dangling from the light bulb, and all was dark. Quickly, I changed my clothes and crawled between the clean sheets.

I again prayed and tried to count my blessings, "Many people in this world live in boxes, under bridges, and in subway tunnels, and go to sleep hungry at night. I have plenty to eat, and though squeaky, this is a pretty comfortable bed." Still my tears came burning my cheeks and soaking my pillow. "Please, just help me not to feel so alone," was my last prayer before the grace of sleep.

"Wake up, Carol." I was aware of a warm hand on my shoulder.

"I'm sorry to wake you," Carlene, one of the counselors said. "I'm afraid your peace and quiet have ended. You're about to get some roommates—eighteen to be exact."

As I sat up and reached for my robe, she continued, "The girls in one of the older dorms heard scratching and howling outside of one of the windows. The counselors found some animal tracks outside. Whatever was there was probably scared away, but the girls are afraid. A couple of the younger ones were crying."

Up the stairs and through the door they trooped—all sizes of them dressed with sweatshirts and coats pulled over their pajamas—carrying sleeping bags and pillows.

Carlene and I helped the girls get mattresses and make their beds.

"Don't stay up too long," Carlene called back as she disappeared down the stairs. "Remember, the bell is going to ring at six o'clock in the morning."

Groans and giggles filled the room.

Two girls who remembered me from last summer's camp, lit on the foot of my bed and relayed the night's adventure. The scare was over and high spirits restored. One of the campers sitting on my cot gave me a hug and said, "Thank you for letting us come up and stay with you. We're sure glad you did!"

Giggling and bed squeaking continued until the light was turned off, but eventually the commotion ceased, and silence again returned to the old dormitory. I even felt like laughing as the girls' infectious spirits attacked my gloom.

I flipped my pillow over to the dry side and snuggled down to sleep assured that God had heard my prayer.

Whatever happened in the week ahead, I knew I was not alone.

The Life-Giving Gift

Regina Moser

The blood drive at church arrived. I hurried over after a long day at work half hoping my blood would prove to be iron deficient as it had a time or two in the past, and I wouldn't have to give. I hurriedly filled out the form and made all sorts of errors that the technician had to double check with me. As I waited for the tests to be run, my mother came into my mind. She had received so much blood and plasma as she fought lymphoma. Her life had been extended and she lived her last days with energy because so many people gave the life-giving gift of blood.

When the nurse came to mark my vein and to swab for exactly thirty seconds with iodine before sliding the needle into my vein, she asked, "Are you comfortable? Do you have any pain? Five minutes is a long time to feel pain." And I think, *Five minutes is such a short period of time in comparison to what my mother endured.* The nurse shakes the bag of blood as it begins to fill up and says, "It looks good, and I realize that this is a time to pray. As my blood goes out of my body, I pray that it will be a life-giving force, a gift to someone in need. I pray for health and healing for the one who will receive my blood. I pray and time passes swiftly. Soon the bag is full and I am left alone to rest for a few moments. When I get up and feel my energy renewed. No longer am I tired after my long day. Giving of myself through action and prayer can restore both the one who gives and the one who receives."

A Face in the Crowd

L. Robert Oaks

It began as the kind of day one prefers to forget. I slept through the alarm, then bolted down a cup of hot tea and some toast, barely making the commuter bus that took me to the train station. There had been no time for a morning prayer for strength for the tasks of the day. Storm clouds gathered overhead, adding to my sense of gloom.

The bus dawdled in the heavy rush-hour traffic. My New York City subway train was also held up for precious minutes while policemen summoned an ambulance team to carry out a man who had fallen ill. My thoughts were less of compassion for the stricken man than concern for the delay in meeting my friend for some work on a book we were writing together. I knew he would be upset at my tardiness, for he had an important appointment later in the day.

As I anticipated, he was annoyed, so our attempt to work together that day seemed futile. We ended early with only one page of progress made. As I left his apartment building, a driving wind made me wish I had worn a scarf and a warmer coat. I hurried to keep warm and to catch the next train from Grand Central Station.

Just then, as she came toward me, I saw the face of an elderly woman and it was filled with pain, frustration, and despair. Slowly, painfully, she took one step after another, carefully lifting ahead of her a four-legged walker. Inwardly and impulsively, I said a prayer. "Dear Lord, the only thing I know I can do for that woman is to pray for her. She needs Your help badly. Give her the strength to persevere and the sense of victory that comes from overcoming pain. Thank You, Lord."

I turned to watch her for a moment before she became lost in the crowd. Did she suddenly walk straighter? Was there a new determination in her face? Or was it just my imagination?

I don't really know, but I do know that in that moment all my own feelings of irritation and frustration seemed to leave me. A warm glow suffused my body, which moments before had been shivering. I continued homeward with a sense of inner peace.

When I turned the key in my own front door, the sweet and pungent fragrance of spareribs drifted in from the kitchen. My wife greeted me with her customary, "How did it go today, dear?"

"It was a good day," I said, giving her a hug. "Let's be thankful!"

CHAPTER 7

For it was you who formed my inward parts;

you knit me together in my mother's womb.

I praise you, for I am fearfully and wonderfully made.

Wonderful are your works; that I know very well.

My frame was not hidden from you,

when I was being made in secret,

intricately woven in the depths of the earth.

Your eyes beheld my unformed substance.

In your book were written all the days

that were formed for me,

when none of them as yet existed.

PSALM 139:13-16 *(NRSV)*

We Are Part of God's Design

I'm never quite sure

whether it's You talking to me,

dear Lord,

or me talking to me.

Keep me from hearing my own voice

when all I want is to listen

to You and only You.

Your plan, Your purpose,

Your will, not mine,

in everything I do.

FAY ANGUS

A Tap on the Window

Suzanne Asplin

Our office is located along a dead-end street. At the very end of that street, there is a single house. That's where Jane and her husband live. One day, I ran into her in the market.

"Hi, Jane. Did you know that our business is now located in the building near your house?" I asked.

"Yes," she replied, "I had heard that."

"I've seen you walk past. Stop in sometime and have a cup of tea with me. I often have free time and would love company."

"Thanks, Sue, I'll do that." It was just a short exchange and we were soon on our separate ways. I had sincerely meant the invitation; however, I doubted that Jane would ever stop in. We were acquainted through mutual friends, but had never had the opportunity to develop a close friendship, so I knew she would be uncomfortable dropping in at my office.

In the coming weeks, each time I saw her walk past the office, I thought I should go out and ask her to come in, but the time was never just right. Sometimes, I was busy with other people, phone calls, or bookkeeping. At other times, I simply hesitated too long and she had gone past.

One particular day, however, I saw Jane walk past my office window, and a few minutes later, walk back in the other direction. Without conscious effort on my part—almost as though someone else was doing it—I simply tapped on the window and beckoned for her to come in. She didn't even hesitate; just looked up, turned, and came in.

I knew there had been many problems and hurts in Jane's life; the most recent being a terrible automobile accident in which her daughter had been seriously injured. A mangled body plus brain damage had kept this young mother hospitalized and comatose for weeks.

After chatting about insignificant matters for a while, I asked how her daughter was doing.

Jane replied, "Alison has made remarkable progress. Her broken bones are mending and she can be up in a wheelchair now. When she came out of the coma, she had the emotional maturity of a two-year-old child, but now has progressed to that of a twelve-year-old. We have reason to expect that she will fully recover. But it is so difficult to deal with a twelve-year-old who is actually twenty-four years old. And Alison's little girl is so confused when her Mommy thinks her daughter is a little friend who has come over to play, or when she is 'tired of playing' and wants to send her 'home.'"

When I asked Jane how she was coping with all this, the tears came out—the fear, the grief, the anger, the hurt, the guilt, the frustrations, the fatigue, the financial strain, the doubts, the questioning.... Jane had reached a very low point where she was questioning why God would allow her to go through one heart-rending circumstance after another; wondering if she were even worthy of calling herself a Christian—surely a "good Christian" wouldn't have to endure all this testing and trauma. Surely others must look at her and wonder why she and her family had to be "pruned" to this extent, and why they had to walk through one "valley" after another.

Having struggled through some difficult years recently myself, I was able to empathize with Jane and share with her some things that had helped me. However, as always when talking with someone who is hurting, I felt so inadequate, so helpless. I could cry with her, I could listen to her, I could pray for her and her family, but I couldn't take away her hurt or ease her pain.

No, I couldn't, but Someone else could. Someone who knew of her doubts, fears, guilt, anger, hurt, and questioning. Someone who knew that she felt He had abandoned her; Someone who knew she needed reassurance that He heard her pleading, saw her tears, and loved her.

For you see, as she was walking—no, she said she was stomping—down the street, she was crying out in her heart to her Lord....

"God, aren't You there anymore?

"God, how can I go on?

"God, it is too much and I feel as though You have left me to handle this all by myself!

"God, don't You love me?

"God, if You love me and if You are there for me, send someone to help me! Someone that I can talk to! Please, Lord.

"I need someone now!"

And then, at that very moment, she heard—a tap on the window.

Prepare for Healing

Phyllis Starling Wallenmeyer

Once again I was curled up in pain. Burning, aching pain was gnawing at my intestines. Fighting chills and nausea, I weakly pulled a comforter up over my shoulders. Powerless to move any further, I fought to concentrate on thoughts other than the spasms that wracked my body.

For twenty-five years I have been fighting pain, infection and inflammation from head to toe, the result of a lifetime fighting Crohn's disease, an inflammatory bowel disease, that first struck when I was just a teenager. I have been hospitalized repeatedly over the decades and I have missed so many wonderful vacations, graduations and celebrations due to the unpredictable nature of this illness. I have turned down jobs, avoided setting appointments and delayed making future plans because I never knew whether I would be well enough to go until the last minute. Even my own wedding was delayed as I suffered through a humiliating four-month flare-up, complete with two months of hospitalization.

I reached over to my bedside table for my latest copy of *Guideposts*. In it was the classic story about a schoolteacher named Marilyn Ludolf with a mysterious illness that had left her face red with searing pockets of boils and inflammation for sixteen years. I, too, often suffered from large inflammatory cysts on my face, in my hair, and on other parts of my body, all thought to be a manifestation of the Crohn's disease. But for me, the most humiliating and crippling symptom was the chronic, unrelenting and often bloody diarrhea. I had always thought that if I could just stop the diarrhea, then the rest of the disease symptoms would be easier to bear.

Like Marilyn, I also felt empathy with the woman in the Bible, who, after suffering from a bleeding disorder for twelve years, touched the hem of Jesus' robe and was healed because of her faith (Mark 5:25-34). I, too, had great faith in God, but I had always wondered in the back of my mind whether it was His will that I have this disease, and perhaps healing would never be possible. In her story Marilyn also questioned whether healing was possible for her. She marked her turning point when she heard a former Miss America, Cheryl Prewitt, proclaim that God had healed her after she prepared herself to be healed. Marilyn then formed her own plan to prepare herself for healing by writing down thirty-six healing scriptures from the Bible, reading and rereading them every waking moment, then confidently setting a date for God to heal her. And He did.

Carefully I turned her words over in my mind. Thousands of times I had prayed for comfort and healing from this dreadful disease, and often I was blessed with temporary relief, but it was always short-lived. Soon the disease would again rear its ugly head and life would crash to a halt while I crept through each day weak from blood and weight loss, pleading silent prayers for help. But I had never specifically prepared myself for healing; I did not even know how. With Marilyn's story as my guide, I, too, began to prepare.

First I wrote down every Bible verse I personally felt moved by which mentioned healing, faith, and giving thanks for answered prayer requests. Then I wrote them together on one page in the form of a prayer and I made many copies putting them every-where: the baby's bag, the car, the kitchen, my desk, my wallet, and my Bible. It had already been a long difficult winter with my current flare-up lasting almost four months. But now, every time I had a spare moment, I reread my prayer until I knew it so well I could silently pray all day long, without ceasing.

The next step was much more difficult. I firmly believe in the power of intercessory prayer and had always asked our church to place my name on the prayer list with every hospitalization, but I had never asked for a specific symptom to be healed by a spe-cific date. This time I was going to boldly and directly ask my friends, relatives and church family to pray specifically for my intestines to heal; to put an end to the lifetime of chronic bloody diarrhea. On June 25th I was scheduled for a colonoscopy at Johns Hopkins Hospital to check the extent of damage to my large intestine after this last, long flare-up and to look for signs of colon cancer. I ended my letters and my own prayers with a request for healing by that date: June 25th.

Directly asking people to pray for me turned out to be much more difficult and humbling than simply asking to be put on a prayer list. My husband and I have a large extended family in many different states; their church families stretch up and down the East Coast and span from Pentecostal Holiness to Unitarian. I felt embarrassed asking everyone I knew to pray a specific prayer for the end of my diarrhea, but finally I sum-moned up my courage and spent weeks making phone calls or writing cards with my request. That in itself turned out to be a wonderful experience. After I learned to set aside my pride it became a joy-filled task akin to sending Christmas cards. I imagined a chorus of constant prayer being sent heavenward for my humble purpose and I felt great love and appreciation for all who helped. I also sent in a prayer request to Guideposts and got back a lovely letter from the person who prayed for me.

I felt on the edge of a precipice. My love of God was deep, and I know He can do great works, but for me to ask for specific healing by a certain date seemed so challenging, almost defiant, not at all modest and Christlike. Even if I did make this special request, there was a very real possibility that this healing was not a part of God's plan for me. Apostle Paul had prayed for healing three times and God had answered no, it was not His will (II Corinthians 12:7-9). I decided to try anyway. I sent my request letters out with a silent prayer for guidance and acceptance for whatever God chose.

Then, a few weeks later, something curious happened. An inspirational book I had just received reminded us to give gifts of kindness to others whenever we can, as God will always return the kindness back to the giver. In that spirit, I gave a book to an acquaintance, who in return, mentioned a health-food cookbook they liked very much and thought might help me. I didn't see much sense in my buying a copy. I could hardly eat anything but mush due to my inflamed intestines, but I went to the library to look it up anyway. While browsing at the library I stumbled on an article that mentioned a physician's success using the old-fashioned BRAT diet (ripe bananas, plain rice, unsweetened applesauce and non-caffeine tea) not just for regular diarrhea, but for chronic diarrhea, too.

Well there was nothing new about the BRAT diet, just about every physician recommends it for diarrhea, but for my chronic disease I thought this was too simple. For most of my life I had tried every imaginable type of diet combination possible, and so I ignored this information. Then I had a dream in which a woman appeared and told me to stop eating certain foods for a while. I ignored this, too. All the while I kept praying, constantly praying. And the dreams kept coming.

One morning after a particularly vivid dream I sat there sleepily and wondered what was going on. I went back to the library and reread the article. I went to the technical reference section and read about my disease and digestion. And then I found it. Information in a textbook that explained what can set off a chronic diarrhea spiral in anyone, regardless of what disease or illness they may have. The text then specifically listed what factors were at work and what needed to be removed to help stop the diarrhea cycle so that rest and medications can work. It not only fit the BRAT diet perfectly, but certain other similar foods as well. I wrote everything down furiously. I wanted to start that very day. At last I felt hope, real hope.

Two days later the chronic diarrhea stopped, completely. It has never returned. On June 25th the colonoscopy showed widespread healing, no colon cancer and no active disease. A second colonoscopy a year later confirmed it. I will always keep my yearly checkups—it's a smart health practice, and I follow other recommendations from my physician, too. I may always be a person diagnosed with Crohn's disease, but I no longer live in fear of diarrhea.

Today I travel extensively and internationally, activities that would have quickly set off flare-ups of diarrhea in the past. I accept work, set appointments, and plan celebrations with confidence. God more than answered my prayers for healing my intestines, He also erased my fears of living fully. The diarrhea may have left me, but the lessons I learned from decades of illness: love, compassion, humility, and thankfulness, will always remain and have made me that much stronger in my faith. God has given me a new life for which I am eternally grateful and I hope to use it to help others facing trials similar to my own.

I certainly have no doubt that God guided me to the information I needed in answer to my prayers for healing, even though it took years. All the while I never gave up my requests, my prayers and my searching. But more importantly, He never gave up on me, in spite of my inability to see that which He kept putting right in front of me. God promises that if we keep asking, then it will be given to us, and if we keep seeking, then we will find what we need (Matthew 7:7). And now I know that whenever I am in need of anything, no matter how impossible it might seem, the first thing to do is to start with a prayer.

Be Available

Joan Clayton

Cody's quiet time every morning includes a simple prayer: "Lord, may I be able to help someone today." Little did Cody know that his prayer would be answered in such a short time.

Cody and his friends were practicing for baseball when he saw it happen. A little boy about five years old was riding a miniature motorcycle across the campus. Cody noticed it because he had never seen a motorcycle so small. The boy was going very slowly and his parents were proudly watching.

The next scene filled them all with horror! The miniature motorcycle began racing at intense speed...faster and faster! The child didn't know what to do, other than to just hang on. As the motorcycle raced toward the brick wall of the school building, the parents started running and screaming. Cody started running too. He was in great physical shape, but he couldn't reach it in time. The motorcycle hit the brick wall, throwing the child in the air.

Cody was there within seconds. He knew the child had to be dead. There was bleeding from the mouth of his pale, motionless body.

It was at this point that Cody yielded to the Greater One in him and relied upon His leading.

"I have a cellular in my car," he said breathlessly as the parents arrive. "I'm going to run to my car and call for an ambulance and the police. Don't move him. Something may be broken."

Cody raced to his car, called the authorities and raced back. The poor parents, understandably, were devastated as they stood crying and wailing. It was then that Cody heard himself speaking these words: "We are going to pray now, and we are going to ask God to be completely in control. We are going to believe Him for taking care of your son. Let's hold hands and surround him.

"Lord, we ask You now to be with this little boy. We place him in Your hands. We ask that You help him and bring him back to wholeness. I pray now for his parents. Please give them peace."

Cody was still praying when the ambulance arrived. Cody kept praying until the ambulance drove away.

That night, Cody tossed and turned, reliving the scene many times. He prayed for the little boy's life throughout the night.

Cody's mom called the surrounding hospitals the next day and located the child and talked to the mother.

"First, let me tell you, little Jackie is going to be all right. He has a broken leg, a bruised lung and a sore tongue. He had bitten his tongue and that was where the bleeding had come from. We believe that your son's prayer not only saved our Jackie, but it also brought my estranged husband and me back together!"

Just a simple prayer Cody had prayed that morning: "Lord, may I be available to help someone today."

Eager Beaver

Peg Joplin

A spring storm had blown down and partially severed two enormous branches from the willow trees on my lakeside property. Hundreds of smaller branches still attached to the larger ones were mired in the muck along the shoreline. I'm responsible for keeping my area neat, so I knew I had a big cleanup to do. But the mess was not accessible from land. I'd have to hire a tree surgeon with a boat, and since I'm a widow living on Social Security, I worried about the expense.

One day I stood surveying the scene. *Dear God,* I prayed, *what am I going to do?* Then I was distracted from my prayer by some beavers, busy felling small trees on the other side of the lake.

The next morning I looked out my window and gasped. The beavers had discovered the half-down branches. I watched as they severed each branch, chewed off the bark, and then headed down the lake with the naked white sticks in their mouths. The urge to go out and cheer them on was strong, but I stayed inside so I wouldn't frighten them away.

All week they worked, and when they were finished, the troublesome branches were gone. In answer to my prayer, God had sent some of his best tree surgeons—a few eager beavers.

A Tire Iron Parable

R. Bruce McPherson

One Chicago morning in early November I was driving north on the Dan Ryan Expressway toward the Loop in our relatively new car, alone with my thoughts and National Public Radio.

Suddenly my right-rear tire exploded. I managed, somehow, to work my way to the left lane and then onto the narrow shoulder of the dangerous roadway, just south of 63rd Street. I climbed carefully out of the car to assess my situation. Cars whirled by at what now were frightening speeds, only six or eight feet from me. I opened the trunk to discover, to my horror, that the full-sized spare tire apparently had not been inflated and that the tire iron was missing. Why hadn't I checked more carefully when I purchased the car? But now it was too late. I was in a proverbial pickle. Towing would be my only resort. I tied my handkerchief to the radio aerial and eased my way back into the car to wait. I wasn't sure what would happen next.

The first car that stopped—no easy task on this section of highway, where one must pull over, stop, and then back up for at least a hundred yards down a perilous shoulder—was driven by a young African American woman. I explained my situation. She said, "I still have some time before I have to be at work. I'll get off and call a tow truck for you."

I thanked her, and she was gone. A second car with a rescuer was driven by a young African American man. I explained that help was on the way, or at least I thought so. "Thanks anyway." He grinned and headed back into the wicked traffic.

The third car that stopped was driven by a burly young African American man in a leather jacket; he looked like a linebacker, but there was a gentleness in his eyes that was impossible to miss. He assessed the situation with me. "I have a spare," he said. I was dumbfounded. He was offering me his spare. So, together, working with his jack and tire irons, we removed my destroyed tire, sharing the roadside danger together. But his spare was too small to fit on my car. He asked, "Is your spare flat or does it just need air?" I said that I thought it was the latter. "I'll go get some air in it for you," he said matter-of-factly, moving quickly and confidently, leaving his jack and tools with me. Off he drove. Ten minutes later he was back. "You're right, all it needed was air." He quickly placed the spare on my car, and I was ready to move again.

With the November wind (better known in Chicago as The Hawk) biting us and the sounds of traffic cascading around us, I found myself a bit tongue-tied. "I can't thank you enough. Can I reimburse you for your time and trouble? Is there something I can do?"

"Yeah. Send me a Christmas card," my hero said, with a touch of a smile on his strong face.

A city tow truck pulled up across the highway. Recognizing that I was in good hands and about to continue my journey, the driver moved on down the road. I like to think that the young woman's phone call was successful.

I found a pen and a piece of paper, and as he was writing down his name and address, I remarked, "You are really a Good Samaritan."

His eyes caught mine. For the first time there was a musing quality to his voice.

"I haven't heard that story mentioned in a long time." He threw his jacket and tools into his car trunk, and he was away. Within minutes I was continuing my trip north, shaken but moving—and moved, too, to reflection and gratitude.

What is worth noting is this reaching out of three citizens to help another in distress, across the constraints of age and race in a city that often makes these variables divisive. As I neared the Loop, I thought of how insignificant public policy is without the capacity of human beings to make life in a city civilized and moral and satisfying.

An older white man was in trouble. Three young African Americans came to him with assistance—simply because they are good people, and a fellow human being needed their help. There, for an hour, at the edge of the Dan Ryan Expressway, the city was not in trouble. It worked for all of us in ways that I still struggle to understand fully, but for which I am enormously grateful.

"What goes around comes around." I have heard my African American friends and colleagues use this phrase over the years. Never did the words have so much meaning. I must redouble my efforts to reach out, too, to my fellow citizens and neighbors who are African American and Hispanic, when I can be the rescuer rather than the rescued.

That year I sent my Good Samaritan a humorous Christmas card. It displayed a car with a Christmas tree on top and a dog sitting in the driver's seat. I felt I had to send a card that involved an auto. I wished him well.

A few days before Christmas a card from him arrived in my mailbox. Inside the card I read this verse from Ecclesiastes 4:9-10 *(NEB)*:

"Two are better than one; they receive a good reward for their toil, because, if one falls, the other can help his companion up again; but alas for the man who falls alone with no partner to help him up."

I deduce from the card that my Good Samaritan is a Christian and a nurse. I began to wonder if the hands of God were on my shoulders. Perhaps that windy November day my car was not on the road to Chicago, but rather toward my own Damascus.

The Prayer Peacock

Dorothy Shellenberger

In the Ozark Mountains west of Eureka Springs, Arkansas, is one of the most beautiful little chapels in the world. It is called Thorncrown Chapel, an architectural wonder made of glass. When I went to see this unique blending of nature and human genius that looks as if it has just grown there in the woods, I met Jim Reed (now deceased), and the schoolteacher who had envisioned this little jewel in the trees. He told me this story:

When we first finished Thorncrown, we encountered a problem that seemed insurmountable. Spiders loved to weave their webs high up in the glass loft of the chapel. Though we cleaned persistently, we couldn't get rid of them. Finally, we turned to the Lord in prayer.

Less than a week later, a full-grown male peacock came to Thorncrown. He just appeared and adopted us. We contacted farmers in the area and even advertised in the local paper, but no one claimed him. We named him Caleb, for he took over our mountain. Besides the grain we fed him, he ate bugs off the ground—including ants and spiders.

One day we realized there were fewer spider webs in the loft than before. Soon there were none at all! All the while we were praying for a solution to our spider problem, Caleb had been at work reducing the spider population!

When Caleb first appeared, did the folks at Thorncrown consider him an answer to prayer? I think not. But God sometimes has a delightful, almost humorous way of performing His wonders. To me the moral of this little peacock story is plain: *Don't be afraid or shy about asking God for anything.* "Ask, and it shall be given you" (Matthew 7:7).

And when you've asked, watch for answers like Caleb. Unlikely and unexpected though they are, they may go a long way toward clearing the "cobwebs" that block your view!

The Struggling Sea Gull

J. Jerome Smith

On a lovely Sunday morning in August my nine-year-old daughter and I were surf fishing in the warm, waist-deep coastal waters about one hundred yards off a tiny island in the Gulf of Mexico. Although we were catching speckled trout abundantly, Katheryne insisted that we stop fishing and wade over to the island to pick up some seashells. Reluctantly, I promised her that after landing two more fish we could go. After stashing three more fish in the creel, I was reminded once again of my promise, and obediently followed her to the beach. Wading ashore, she marveled at the abundance of seashells and hermit crabs that adorned the sands of this little barrier island beach. She scrambled about in wide-eyed wonder, happily filling both hands to overflowing with shells. I spotted an empty plastic gallon jug, cut off the top, and brought it to her to store her growing new seashell collection.

As we continued to move down the island, hundreds of sea gulls were startled by our presence and hastily flew away. However, there before us was a very young sea gull who remained. He was trying to fly away but could not. Something was wrong. Every time the young creature attempted to take off, he would reach an altitude of about twelve inches, then abruptly fall back to the sand. The frantic gull did this repeatedly, with increasing frequency, as we approached. Then Katheryne asked, "Daddy, what's wrong with that bird?" I replied, "Looks like it might have a broken wing. If so, I'm afraid it's going to die of hunger, since it won't be able to glide over the waters to scoop up little fish."

As we got nearer, however, it was obvious that his wings were okay, but there was something else wrong. I reached down for the bird only to find out that it had become entangled in fishing line. Gingerly I cupped the little fellow in my hands and picked him up. This is the first time the poor bird had been touched by a human, I remember thinking as I felt its pulse racing in fear. No wonder it's scared to death. Using the fingernail clippers that hung from my neck, I clipped the clear fishing line knotted around its left foot and lifted the bird upward toward the heavens. As I opened my hands, the bird flew off. We both watched it as it sped for the horizon, and when we could no longer see it, I glanced down at my little girl and said, "Now, Katheryne, this bird is free and will live. If we hadn't come along and helped, he would surely have died." The smile that spread on her face told me how proud she was of what we had done. It was such a special feeling that the two of us had shared. And that sweet and innocent smile of hers was more reward than I could have ever hoped for, having stopped fishing those few magic moments to follow her to that enchanted stretch of seashore. What a delight...to watch her excitedly gather seashells with a child's sense of excitement and innocent wonder that seems to evade us as we grow older...to see her face after the little gull soared up into the sky, free from the bondage of the fishing line, with another chance at life!

We continued to stroll down the beach, and several moments later she shouted, "Look Daddy, there's the sea gull we helped!"

as the bird flapped over our heads. I turned to her and said, "Yeah, I guess he came back just to say "Thank you for helping me."

That special moment that God granted me and my daughter that golden, unforgettable Sunday morning danced in my mind for the remainder of the day, and right through church that same evening. In fact, I couldn't put the vision of that bird out of my mind, nor get the lump out of my throat. In prayer, I pondered with joy the truth that God really created fish to swim, birds to fly…and human beings to share in God's glory on earth, and more fully some day in heaven. God offers us freedom to be happy, joyful, childlike, and peace-filled, if only we will open our hearts to His ineffable grace, and surrender our lives completely to God. The elation that suffuses our being when we allow God to sever those binding strings of attachment to the world and its mundane concerns can be described only as *true freedom.* Absent that release from attachments, our souls certainly will starve, because we cannot be nourished with divine life while hopelessly tethered to the earth.

After service, I wrote the following prayer:

Today, dear Lord, I thank You for following my child and me along one of life's shores to discover a grace-filled mystery that still warms my heart in the memory. I thank You for allowing me to see myself in that young sea gull that morning.

Reflecting back, I recall the countless times I was hopelessly strapped to this earth, just like the poor bird…and despite strong resolve and effort, was helpless to break loose from the ties that bound me.

Each time I struggled to rise above my earthly attachments, concerns, afflictions, sorrows, worries, or limitations, I invariably faltered and fell...just like the little sea gull. I am so grateful You stayed beside me during my own struggles and never gave up on me. I bow my head and offer a prayer of humble thanksgiving for Your part in "cutting my invisible strings" and letting me soar freely, just like the little sea gull. Yet again Your gentleness and inspiration overwhelm me, and the simple ways You use to reach this man, who continues searching for You in the complexity of his daily existence on this earth, never fail to humble me. I stand before You truly blessed, and thankful now to be free, because of Your love for me...just like the little sea gull.

Letters to Prayer Fellowship

As you read these words, thousands of hurting and frightened people who are facing hard times are posting prayer requests on the Guideposts Web Site, mailing a letter or making a phone call to Guideposts Prayer Fellowship. Those in need are tapping in to the power of prayer.

We've decided to let some of those who have contacted Guideposts asking for prayer in recent months to have the last word. As you read these final testimonies to answered prayer, let them prompt you to pray and reach out to others who are in need of help. Who knows? You may be God's answer to somebody's prayer.

I am not one to leave my problems at work. The first weekend in May I went on a retreat. I had a terrible day at work on the previous Thursday and wanted to quit my job. I came home Sunday, and in my mail was a book from Guideposts. I saw the blurb about writing you for prayer. I wrote you, but never mailed the letter. The following week at work, all of a sudden things seemed different. We were being civil to each other and actually working together! **—S.K.**

I am writing to update you about a friend of mine for whom you were recently asked to pray—a young wife, pregnant, whose amniotic sac was ruptured during her sixth month. She was told the fetus would not be able to proceed through the normal development process.

One week after your prayer session, the baby has tripled its weight, turned from breech to a normal birth position in the womb and doubled her lung capacity. Doctors are shocked. I would like to thank you (as well as our God). I'm sure the baby thanks you also.

Because I attribute this miracle to the power of prayer, I ask you to pray for another friend of mine, a fellow nursing school graduate who has failed state boards three times.

I don't ask you to pray for a passing grade, but that God will fill her with the Holy Spirit, helping her to have faith in God and His will for her. I believe that if she will just turn this over to God, she will achieve the success she has worked so hard for. **—C.N.**

I'd like to share our praise and thanksgiving for answered prayer. My brother-in-law was diagnosed with a brain tumor. Surgery was done and instead of the tumor expected, they found a fluid filled sack. We are relieved and thankful, and request prayer for Don and his family, for closeness to God and awareness of His love for each of them. **—H.M.**

I just want to say thanks to those who are praying with me for my marriage. Last night (Saturday the 17th) was the first time I talked to my ex-husband in over a year. It was only for a very short time, but there were no bad words or hurt feelings when I left him in that parking lot. I had a peace that was so wonderful, anyone that has ever had it knows what I am talking about. I still have it today. Thanks. **—L.R.**

I want to thank God for the gift of pregnancy. Three years ago I had surgery that almost claimed both ovaries, but God had other plans. My husband is adopted and this will be his first child. Steven and I will be married two years on Monday, and "Emory" is due to join our family in July. I have a daughter that will be ten in June. We are a lower middle class family that requires both parents to work. My prayer request has been answered. My job is allowing me time off to stay home with our baby, three months full-time and part-time at home and part time at the office until the baby is six months old. —**E.W.**

God Does Answer Prayers! Thank You Everyone For Your Prayers! I have been praying and waiting. The Lord answers prayer in His own time. The last year has not been easy, but God has once again blessed me with His wisdom. In my time of need, He was always there and He sent a special angel to help me. Her name is Laurie. By sending Laurie, God taught me many things. If times are hard for you now, and your prayers do not seem like they are being answered, Do Not Quit Praying. God is there and is listening. God Does Care. —**S.S.**

Several months ago, my husband and I both left our jobs at the same company where we had worked for the past fourteen years. Changes in the employer's policies, philosophies and their treatment of the employees made it necessary for us to make this "leap of faith." Our departure was preceded by many months of prayer for guidance and wisdom. Then, one day, it was over.

During the ensuing days that turned into weeks, and then months, we experienced many ups and downs. It was during one of these "down" moments that I logged on to Guideposts' prayer request page. What I found there was a place where I could lay my troubles aside. Certainly, these people had greater difficulties than we were experiencing. I found myself reading and praying for all of them.

In time, we both found new employment. We are not earning as much as we were, but we are much happier. The future beckons with possibilities and we have faith that the Lord will fill in the gaps between our income and our expenses. This morning I would like to share my journal entry of gratitude with anyone who ever feels a lack of faith.

"Friday, June 11: Thank you Lord, once again! You have answered our prayers. How can I begin to express my gratitude? Nothing I could say or do would be enough. You have given us all that we desired and more. We are humbled by Your generosity and ashamed by our many doubts and fears along the path. Will we never learn to completely "Let go and let God?" That will be my goal every day for the remainder of my life.

Bless me and mine this day, dear Lord. We are forever in need of Your guiding presence. Keep our paths straight, I pray, even when we are blind to Your light. Open our eyes to Your love and glory. Amen."

It is my hope, in sharing this note of gratitude, that your readers will find a deeper faith in God's purpose in their lives. We can never know what the future holds. We can only know that our faith in God makes all things possible.   **—D.M.**

A NOTE FROM THE EDITORS

This original Guideposts book was created by the Book and Inspirational Media Division of the company that publishes *Guideposts*, a monthly magazine filled with true stories of people's adventures in faith.

Guideposts is available by subscription. All you have to do is write to Guideposts, 39 Seminary Hill Road, Carmel, New York 10512. When you subscribe, each month you can count on receiving exciting new evidence of God's presence, His guidance and His limitless love for all of us.

Guideposts is also available on the Internet by accessing our home page on the World Wide Web at www.guideposts.org. Send prayer requests to our Monday morning Prayer Fellowship. Read stories from recent issues of our magazines, *Guideposts, Angels on Earth, Guideposts for Kids*, and *Guideposts for Teens*, and follow our popular book of devotionals, *Daily Guideposts*. Excerpts from some of our best-selling books are also available.

My Answered Prayers

My Answered Prayers

My Answered Prayers